the complete guide to

buying & selling property

2ND EDITION

DAILY ✠ EXPRESS

the complete guide to
buying & selling
property 2ND EDITION

sarah o'grady

**KOGAN
PAGE**

For my family

Publisher's note
Every possible effort has been made to ensure that the information contained in this book is accurate at the time of going to press, and the publishers and authors cannot accept responsibility for any errors or omissions, however caused. No responsibility for loss or damage occasioned to any person acting, or refraining from action, as a result of the material in this publication can be accepted by the publisher, the author or Express Newspapers.

For ease of expression only, the male pronoun has generally been used throughout this book.

First published in Great Britain in 2003 by Kogan Page Limited
Second edition 2004

120 Pentonville Road
London N1 9JN
www.kogan-page.co.uk

© Express Newspapers 2003
© Sarah O'Grady and Kogan Page 2004

British Library Cataloguing in Publication Data

A CIP record for this book is available from the British Library

ISBN 0 7494 4194 1

Typeset by Saxon Graphics Ltd, Derby
Printed and bound in Great Britain by Cambrian Printers Ltd, Aberystwyth, Wales

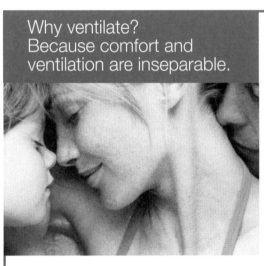

Waring helps you cook up a treat

For a range of kitchen essentials that offers both unparalleled performance and undisputed style, look to Waring from New Classics Ltd.

If you want to be able to whiz up healthy smoothies or devilish cocktails from the comfort of your own home, plump for the Original Retro Blender by Waring. First manufactured in the 1930s, this blender is built to last but does not cut corners on style. Available in a choice of seven classic finishes.

For maximum versatility, try the sleek SmartPower Duet Blender/ Processor. With its 5 powerful speed settings, chic chromed base and graduated heat resistant blending jug, you get both practicality and designer flare for your money. And, because the Duet comes complete with its own processing bowl and blades, you get two appliances for the price of one!

For tasty yet tasteful toast day after day, choose Waring's new four-slot toaster in satin stainless steel. Thanks to its independent browning controls and four self-centring racks, it can handle everything from bread and bagels to crumpets and teacakes with ease.

For multi-tasking, nothing tops the functional yet fashionable Mini-Prep Plus food processor. This dinky appliance features the new auto-reversing SmartPower blade, which spins anti-clockwise to chop or puree with the sharp edge, or clockwise to grind spices with the dull edge.

And, as everyone knows, cordials can never compete with the taste of fresh, unadulterated juice. Cue Waring's Health Juice Extractor and commercial quality Juicerator. Both appliances are easy to clean and offer a great shortcut to upping your daily vitamin intake.

For further information on all of the above, and more, call New Classics direct on
01707 265465.

Contents

Contents

IMPROVE THE CHANCES OF SELLING YOUR HOME

Use SELF STORAGE for your clutter. As identified on all popular T.V. home mover programmes

Three ways Spaces Personal Storage can assist your sale:

BEFORE YOU MOVE

According to channel 5's "House Doctor" Ann Maurice, the use of self storage in order to get all the clutter out of the home, not only makes the house look considerably bigger, but also enables the potential purchaser to visualise their furniture and possessions in the house.

Why not tidy away some of your bulkier cumbersome furniture in a small storage room at Spaces Personal Storage when you put your home up for sale? There is no charge for access so you can come and go as often as you like to add or retrieve your goods.

MAKING THE SALE

Many people accept an offer on their home to avoid getting involved in a chain. They simply rent a property short term and use a self storage room for their household possessions, leaving them to concentrate on house hunting. Remember that unlimited access to your storage room is **free** at Spaces personal storage, unlike traditional removers who pack your goods away in a container and charge you if you need anything.

BUYING THE NEW PROPERTY

If you are buying a house that needs work done to it, rent a self storage room with Spaces to store furniture and belongings whilst you redecorate your new home. Everyone knows how much easier building and decorating work is when a room is empty. There is no chance of damaging anything either.

We make moving easier. For information reservations and advice about your self storage needs, and details regarding our secure storage centres across the country visit our website at **www.spaces.uk.com** or call our reservation centre free on **0800 22 66 44**.

ALL MODERN HOUSES STRUGGLE FOR STORAGE SPACE

For homeowners everywhere, the use of flexible self-storage represents a great way of optimising your available living space.

For instance, you may want to free up space in a spare bedroom that's currently piled high with clutter. Or you may wish to convert existing storage space, such as a loft, to create an extra bedroom, adding real value to your property in the process.

Spaces is the country's largest personal household storage company with centres throughout the UK. At each centre, you'll find the same high standards – clean individual storage rooms within a highly accessible storage environment plus extremely helpful staff. Not to mention 24 hour CCTV, to ensure your possessions stay totally safe and secure while they remain at Spaces.

In fact, more and more people across the country are making the most of the opportunity to use self-storage on an ongoing basis. As one of our customers quoted recently "A friend told me about using self-storage, until then I had never even considered using it. Living in a two bedroom flat with very little storage space it turns out to be the perfect answer to all our problems. We use it as if it's another room in our flat."

The dry, clean, secure units are ideal for storing valued, but space consuming, possessions such as treasured hobby collections, sports equipment, garden equipment and clothes – some customers even use Spaces to store cars! Simply put, whatever it is you're looking to store, if you haven't got space, you've always got Spaces.

For information reservations and advice about your self storage needs, and details regarding our secure storage centres across the country visit our website at **www.spaces.uk.com** or call our reservation centre free on **0800 22 66 44.**

Introduction

I want readers of this book to feel that they have their own property expert at their side as they navigate the maze that is the British property market.

Written in plain and simple language, I've packed the pages with practical information aimed at making your life as a home-buyer and owner as easy, enjoyable and stress-free as possible.

As buying or selling a house is likely to be the biggest financial transaction most of us are involved in, the stakes are high. Without careful planning or clear thought, buying a property can turn into a nightmare of gargantuan proportions. In fact, moving home has been ranked with death and divorce as one of the top causes of stress in our lives. Surveys and solicitors fees aren't cheap and one mistake can cost you thousands of pounds. And the effort of house-hunting, packing and unpacking, as you stumble through the UK's convoluted and old-fashioned system of purchasing property is likely to add grey hairs.

Whether you are a first-time buyer, a serial mover or an amateur landlord, you will, I hope, find the answers to most of your questions within these pages.

1

Can you afford to buy and what are the first steps?

Just like having your own property expert at your side, this book provides invaluable help at every twist and turn of the property maze. I've covered all the essential topics like knowing what to look for when you first see a property; demystifying estate agents' jargon; understanding what your solicitor should be doing for you; and choosing the right mortgage for your lifestyle. And, once you've finally moved in, hopefully this book will help you to make the most of your investment and make your property as attractive as possible to future buyers. Packed to the brim with practical and accessible information and insider know-how, *The Complete Guide to Buying and Selling Property* guides you safely through the UK property market and will help make your move, and your career as a homeowner, as enjoyable and stress-free as possible.

For many people, the question, 'Can I afford to buy my own home?' really should be: 'Can I afford *not* to buy?'

Renting is fine if interest rates are high or threaten to rise steeply, or if you have other doubts about your future career path. Compared to renting, however, buying a property makes more economic sense in the long-term.

Issues to consider

The following are some key points to consider:

■ How much is the mortgage compared to the cost of renting?

■ At what level would interest rates have to rise for renting to make more sense?

■ How much more would I have to pay in terms of household and other insurance, annual maintenance costs, service charges (where applicable) and any other costs?

■ What are the up-front costs of buying (legal and mortgage application fees, surveys, stamp duty)?

■ If I am taking out an interest-only loan, could I afford to pay into a separate investment plan to pay off the loan itself?

■ Am I going to lose any flexibility to move – perhaps to further a career or travel?

Of course, people buy and sell for all kinds of reasons, not just because it's economically a better deal. Sometimes, as the bills and fees mount up, it is obviously not.

While I am strongly in favour of owning my own home – along with more than 70 per cent of the UK population that does so – I am not in favour of personal bankruptcy. If you can save a larger deposit while paying rent for a few months longer, then do so. That will save you more money in the long run – as the bigger the deposit, the less interest you pay – and will give you a greater choice of property when you start looking around.

How difficult can it be?

Listening to the conversation at any dinner party, a novice buyer can be forgiven for thinking that buying a property is easy. Simply find the right house, spend the most money you've ever spent on what will probably be your biggest purchase ever and wait for move-in day. Right? Wrong.

As those of us who have had our fingers burnt – sometimes more than once – know, buying your own home can be a supremely satisfying achievement. Or, it can be a most frustrating, disappointing, stressful, emotional and expensive episode. The secret between one and the other lies in proper prior planning.

Proper prior planning

Don't walk into any old estate agent's office on the High Street, arrange to view and then make an offer on the first place you see. Ask around for local recommendations of agents in the area you want to move to.

Visit the ones that have been recommended. How do they strike you? Are they members of the National Association of Estate Agents (NAEA). Membership of the NAEA means they have signed up to a Code of Practice and professional Rules of Conduct. This does not guarantee good service or honest dealing, but does give you some leverage if things go wrong. Many reputable agents also belong to the Ombudsman for Estate Agents (OEA) scheme.

Remember that an estate agent works for the seller – not you. They earn their commission by helping owners to sell. A reputable and professional agent should always answer your questions truthfully, but they are not obliged to tell you anything negative about the property. That's why you need a good solicitor.

Also, look at the adverts in the local papers – an agent with the wit to run a polished advertising campaign is a better bet than one who places a few grainy photos. While you're in these branches, take away as many details about as many properties in your price range as possible. Study them so you get a good idea of what's on offer and at what kind of price.

Find out how much you can borrow

Arrange at least a couple of appointments with mortgage lenders. Start with the bank or building society you bank with. There's a relationship there already and they have all your financial details to hand.

You need to know exactly how much they will lend you and what kind of deal they will give you. Don't be afraid of asking questions or trying to negotiate a better deal. Competition between lenders is intense. Exploit it. Don't stick with one lender if another is likely to offer you more favourable terms.

There's no charge, so see as many as you like. Don't let them sell you anything – insurance etc – as there's plenty of time before you're likely to make an offer. Take copious notes.

Also, read the money and personal finance pages of the newspapers. They have up-to-the-minute details of all the latest mortgage offers.

Viewing

Now you're ready to view, there are three golden rules:

- Don't waste the estate agent's time.
- Don't waste the seller's time.
- Don't waste your own time.

If you want a garden flat and the agent offers you a top-floor apartment, don't bother going to see it. If you start by seeing absolutely everything, you'll find yourself harassed and disappointed. Stick within the remit you've set the agent.

Do try and have some idea about the kind of property you're looking for. The agent needs to have some boundaries to work within. If he takes you to see ten or so and you're never interested, he's going to write you off as a waste of time and concentrate on other clients where he's more likely to get a sale.

Questions to ask yourself

The following questions might be useful in narrowing your choice:

I   Do you want a house or a flat?

I   Do you want an old property or a new one?

I   Do you care if the home is leasehold or freehold? Freehold means you own the land on which the house stands and most houses are freehold. Leasehold means you have a lease on a property for a number of years (you can buy properties with leases of just 15 years, but most are hundreds of years long), which is sold to you by the freeholder of the land. That means you own the property but not the land. Most flats, for example, are leasehold.

I   Where do you want to live?

I   Do you want a garden?

I   Do you need parking?

I   Do you need to be close to public transport?

I   How many bedrooms do you want?

I   Do you want to renovate the building or do you want to be able to move straight in?

I   How long are you planning to live in it? Is it suitable if your circumstances change, ie if you have children or an elderly parent moves in?

It's both a strength and a weakness of the way we buy and sell property in England and Wales that a buyer can withdraw right up to the last minute. That's not the case in Scotland where contracts are signed much earlier in the proceedings. But to deliberately string a seller along if you have no real intention of buying is not honourable. Treat others as you would wish to be treated. If you're buying now the chances are that you will be a seller in the future.

Questions to ask the seller

You should ask the seller as many questions as possible when viewing:

I Why are you moving?

I How long has the property been on the market?

I Is it chain-free?

I What are you leaving behind? Are you expecting payment for some of the fixtures, ie carpets?

I How much are the average utility bills?

I How much is the council tax?

I How much is the service charge or ground rent?

I What are the neighbours like?

I Have you ever been burgled?

I Have you made any improvements to the property? Have you got the guarantees and warranties?

I How easy is it to park? Do I need a permit? How much do they cost?

I What are the local schools like?

I Is it a Neighbourhood Watch area?

I What are the local transport links?

I What local amenities – libraries, shops, surgeries – are there?

I Does the area you are looking at carry increased likelihood of flooding or subsidence?

▌ Is there a noisy main road or railway line nearby, or is it in an airport flight path?

Finding a solicitor or licensed conveyancer

So you've found a couple of estate agents you trust, you know how much you can borrow and you're viewing properties. Now find a solicitor or licensed conveyancer to handle any purchase for you.

The best way is by word-of-mouth. Unless you already have a family solicitor, a personal recommendation is worthwhile having. Someone local to the area in which you want to buy is also a good idea, as they will have a better idea of council planning polices or restrictions.

The Law Society, the National Solicitors' Network or the Council for Licensed Conveyancers will also supply you with a list of people practising in your area. Your mortgage lender may also give you a couple of names. Again, you don't have to sign up to anything immediately. You simply want to find someone you trust to do a good job and know how much they're likely to charge in advance of any offer you might make.

Buying a home in England and Wales takes twice as long as in the rest of Europe. Pitfalls such as gazumping – the seller accepting a higher offer after they have already accepted yours – or gazundering – a buyer threatening to withdraw at the last minute unless the seller reduces the price – litter the way.

Proper prior planning means you know what you're talking about and gives you an edge in terms of time. If you have your finances and solicitor sorted out in advance, you can move quicker than your competitors, thereby reducing the risk of losing your dream house.

2 Finding the right area

Finding the right area to live is now far easier than it used to be. With new online services you can compare everything from house prices to a local school's results in seconds.

Issues to consider

When you start looking for a new home there are various factors that could affect your choice of where to live. The list below covers the main considerations.

Schools

If you have a young family, getting your children into the right school can determine the area you choose. Beware, though: school catchment areas are not clearly defined. Check with your estate agent exactly what 'in the vicinity of' (a typical agent's blurb) actually means – and confirm that with the school itself.

Council tax

Living in some areas can seem attractive until the council tax bill comes in and you discover that, in addition to the mortgage, you have to find a further £500–£600 a year. Sometimes it would make more sense to look at a property just a few streets away from your preferred location.

Don't Buy More than Your Bargained For

The house you want to buy may look perfect but how much do you really know about the surrounding area or the land the property is built on? Do you know if your new home is built on a former industrial site that may have left contamination in the ground? Is there a planning application to build a supermarket in the adjoining field? Could your home be at risk from flooding? These are just some of the important questions you should consider when buying a new home.

The consequences of buying a property affected by environmental risks can be serious and expensive. Your property value can be substantially reduced if the land it's built on is contaminated, liable to flooding or affected by other environmental risks. Whilst serious problems are rare, it now costs so little to check on a whole series of potential problems that many homebuyers are asking their solicitor for an environmental search as a matter of course.

Your solicitor will usually undertake a local search as part of the conveyancing process but this will not tell you anything about environmental problems or future developments in the locality that could affect the property. In order to protect your investment and to avoid any nasty surprises it's worth asking your solicitor or licensed conveyancer to commission an Envirosearch and Plansearch report.

Envirosearch, approved by the NHBC, provides essential information on environmental risks including landfill and waste sites, contamination, polluting processes, hazardous substances, radioactive substances, mining activity, subsidence, flooding, radon and transmitters. Envirosearch also includes a surveyor's opinion that comments on whether the property value is likely to be affected by land contamination. Additionally Envirosearch provides a contaminated land insurance option to protect against unknown risks from contamination.

Plansearch provides homebuyers with details of current and historical planning applications for the property and the surrounding area. The report also provides details on future planning proposals in your neighbourhood as well as flood risk information. This report goes much further than the standard local authority search, which provides planning information just on an individual property.

Envirosearch and Plansearch will help any homebuyer to make an informed decision about purchasing a property and whether it will provide a suitable environment and investment for their family. Envirosearch is priced £39 and Plansearch costs £30 however you can save yourself £10 if you order both reports together. A small price to pay for peace of mind.

Do you know what your house is built on?

If you think your tax is too high, write to the council immediately. Challenging a council tax valuation on your property is generally possible only shortly after purchase, although there may be exceptions.

The 50 per cent rebate on council tax for second homeowners has been scrapped and owners can be liable for up to 90 per cent of the local rate.

Services

Not only can council taxes be high, services such as rubbish collection, road mending, sports facilities and parks may be inadequate. Check them out, together with other amenities, such as cinemas, shops and restaurants. Decide whether they meet your current and likely future needs.

Transport

Transport links are an important consideration. Prices are usually lower in areas with poor links, but that is not an inviolable rule. If you are buying in London, check the boundaries of the Congestion Charge.

Conservation area

Conservation areas are 'areas of special architectural or historic interest, the character of which it is desirable to preserve or enhance'. Or at least that's the official definition. Most home-buyers know that conservation areas are more expensive to buy in as properties are generally more sought after. Most importantly of all, if you have any plans to extend, develop, refurbish or convert, any work done on a house in a conservation area will come under the spotlight from both neighbours and local planners anxious to preserve the character of the place. There are more than 9,000 conservation areas in England and the number is increasing.

Crime

A home can turn into a prison if you live in a heavily crime-ridden area. Find out from your local police station what the crime statistics are or look at the local authority website. Talk to local shopkeepers to learn more. Consider personal safety issues, such as whether this is an area you would feel comfortable walking around at night or when coming home from work.

House prices

In the past couple of years, parts of the UK have seen spectacular rises in property values. Other areas of the country have languished. Many big cities have seen double-digit price increases, while others have stood still. Your first need is for a roof over your head. But after that, there's nothing wrong with trying to find the latest hotspot.

To find a future hotspot, where prices are set to rise faster than average, check for emerging developments in the area. For example, is it close to another area that is over-heating where you might benefit from over-spill purchases? Are new transport links planned?

How to buy a home in a sought-after area

If your heart is set on moving into a particular neighbourhood, you may find that you are not the only one who absolutely must have a home there.

For whatever reason, be it the best schools, the nicest streets, the choice of restaurants on the doorstep or the exclusive postcode, sought-after areas present a real challenge to the house hunter and proper prior planning is the key.

Networking

Before a property ever makes it as far as the estate agent's shop window or newspaper advertisement, it's been seen by a huge number of people. Some properties in areas of high demand never even appear on the open market, as professional house hunters and corporate relocation agents make it their business to be on the agent's priority list, so they get the inside track on new properties coming up for sale. You, too, need to make those kind of contacts, so that if a desirable property comes on the market you get an early tip-off.

Visit the local estate agents to introduce yourself. Find the one or two who deal most in the kind of property you want to buy in the area you like. Make sure the agents know you are not a time-waster. Impress upon them that you are a serious buyer with the ability to move quickly if the right kind of property comes up. Telephone or drop in regularly so they have your face and requirements in mind as new homes come on the market.

Check what day the property pages are published in the local paper. It may be possible that the newsagent can forward them on to you. Check out the local property website.

Visit the area regularly. You may find For Sale boards being put up that day, or people moving out.

Mail shot the houses in the neighbourhood you want to move into. If you have a PC and printer, it is easy to knock up a leaflet. Posting, say, 80 of them on a Saturday morning might turn up a surprising result and even if the house owner isn't moving, they may know someone who is.

Preparation

As soon as you have made the decision to move and found the right area, do as much preparation as possible. Good preparation will enable you to make better decisions about properties and move quicker.

Make a wish list of what you want from a property, the features you must have and the things you can live without. This will help focus your mind on the types of property you want and help you filter out those properties that you could get carried away with.

Arrange a provisional mortgage offer first and start talking to a solicitor. The more paperwork you have sorted out, the quicker you can proceed when your offer has been accepted.

Viewings

You must be ready to move quickly in sought-after areas. If an agent calls and says 'I've just had this wonderful flat come on the market', you need to be able to say, 'Great, I'm on the way.' Failing that, make arrangements for someone whose opinion you trust to do the viewing, perhaps with a camcorder if you have access to one, so you can view the pictures later. Take a notebook with you to make notes. Try and imagine the room without the seller's furniture in it. Look at the physical aspects of the property – not the seller's taste. Are the rooms large enough? Do they get enough light? Is there room to extend the kitchen, etc?

What kind of property do you want?

Buying old

Many of us harbour a love of older houses with their in-built character. Whether they are Edwardian villas in the city or listed Georgian rectories in the country, these kinds of properties are sought-after, as generations of new owners imagine the lives of the people who lived in the house before them.

The best of the UK's older properties – 550,000 of them ranging from cottages to castles – are classified as part of the country's heritage and are listed Grade I, Grade II* and Grade II.

All buildings built before 1700 that survive in anything like their original condition are automatically listed, as are many built in the 18th, 19th and even the 20th century.

Properties are listed because:

▌ they are of special architectural interest;

▌ they are of special historical interest;

▌ they have close historical associations with nationally important events or people;

▌ they have special historical or architectural importance as a group of buildings;

▌ they are considered to be of outstanding design or quality; or

▌ they mark a pinnacle of building fashion or standards.

The most important structures are listed Grade I, including Windsor Castle and the Houses of Parliament, and there are nearly 9,000 of them. But if you are lucky enough to be thinking of buying a Grade I listed building, do bear in mind that ownership comes with responsibilities and restrictions. Nothing can be done to alter the building and all repairs have to be carried out in keeping with the original. Because of this, repairs and maintenance can be cripplingly expensive. In some cases, however, grants are available from English Heritage to help with the cost.

Grade II is the commonest classification and there are 350,000 Grade II listed buildings in the country. Here, too, owners face restrictions and have to get special consent for alterations to the property.

Local authorities sometimes give grants towards repair work on listed buildings and you save on VAT, which is zero-rated for improvements on approved alterations.

If you fancy owning a piece of history, contact Save Britain's Heritage or the Society for the Protection of Ancient Buildings. In Scotland, contact the Scottish Civic Trust.

Why buy old?

Older homes are more popular:

▌ one in five households (4.2 million) live in houses that were built before 1919;

▌ a house dating from before 1919 is worth, on average, some 20 per cent more that an equivalent house from a more recent era. This premium rises to 34 per cent for a seventeenth-century period house; and

▌ a survey by MORI of London residents suggested that the most popular choice of home was a 'pre-war semi-detached house with garden'.

Older homes can be cheaper to maintain:

▌ new research by English Heritage suggests that older homes can be more cost-effective and sustainable to maintain over the longer-term;

▌ a Victorian terraced house is cheaper to maintain over a 100-year period than a house built in the 1980s; and

▌ the reason for this is the greater quality and durability of materials used in the construction of older houses, and the higher standards of their design and construction compared to some modern homes.

Using older homes will contribute to sustainability policies:

▌ re-use of older housing stock has an important part to play in building sustainable communities;

▌ the cost of keeping a Victorian terraced house in Nelson West, Lancashire, in a habitable quality for a 30-year period has been estimated at £24,600, compared to the £64,000 that it would cost to demolish that house, replace it with a new house and then maintain that modern home over the same period;

▌ the total energy that has already been used in the construction of a typical Victorian terrace is equivalent to the amount of energy (in fuel terms) that could drive a car five times round the earth or half the distance from the earth to the moon. Retaining and reusing the existing building stock prevents that energy from being wasted and increases resource productivity;

▌ older homes are more likely to suffer from neglect and decay (some 5 per cent of pre-1919 dwellings currently lie vacant compared with less than 3 per cent of properties built since then) but imaginative approaches are possible that would retain the character of older homes while making them fit for modern living;

▌ new houses were built at an average rate of 140,000 per year between 1996 and 2001, in the same time only 20,000 new houses per year resulted from the re-use or conversion of existing housing stock.

Buying new

New homes are increasing in popularity as developers shrug off their old reputations for boring, box-like homes built without character or style, and build exciting, innovative homes for families in the 21st century.

A new home has all kinds of advantages: high-tech heating and lighting systems, high security, luxurious fixtures and fittings, modern plumbing and all 'mod cons' in the bathrooms and kitchens.

If you get in to a new development early enough – perhaps by buying 'off-plan' before the property is even built – many developers offer buyers the opportunity to choose their own fixtures, fittings and colour schemes.

You must make sure though, that you buy a property that has been built by one of the 20,000 companies that are members of the National House Building Council (NHBC), or those that are members of the Zurich Municipal Scheme, which means that the building of the property is insured against the developer going bankrupt. Major defects found in the first two years will also be put right.

There are very few lenders who will give you a mortgage on a property that is not built by an NHBC or Zurich builder or under the supervision of a properly insured architect or surveyor.

NHBC and its Buildmark cover for new homes

NHBC is the leading warranty and insurance provider for new homes in the UK. Established over 65 years ago, NHBC's primary purpose is to raise standards in the house-building industry and provide consumer protection for new homebuyers in the form of the ten year Buildmark warranty.

NHBC raises standards for UK's new homebuyers in a number of ways including registering builders who agree to comply with NHBC's Rules and Standards, setting construction standards for new homes and inspecting at key stages of construction.

1.6 million homes are currently covered by NHBC's Buildmark warranty and in 2003 more than 177,000 Buildmark certificates were issued on new homes.

Buildmark at a glance

1. **Before completion** – This applies even before the home is finished, protecting your deposit if the builder becomes insolvent before the work is completed.

2. **The first two years** – During the first two years the builder is responsible for rectifying any problems or defects which do not comply with NHBC's Technical Standards. If a homeowner and builder cannot agree on what repair work is required, NHBC can offer its free independent Resolution Service and NHBC will instruct the builder to carry out repair works where necessary.

3. **Years three to ten** – For the remaining eight years of the cover the home is covered for damage caused by defects in specific structural areas, as well as elements such as double-glazing, staircases and plastering.

For the whole story on NHBC and Buildmark call **0800 688788** for a brochure and free video or CD-ROM, or visit **www.nhbc.co.uk**

There are a few things worth bearing in mind if you are buying a new-build home.

▌ Check the builder's reputation and look at houses he has built before.

▌ Is he a member of the NHBC? If so, the property qualifies for the Corporation's 10-year Buildmark Cover after completion. Ring 0845 845 6422 to check.

▌ Visit the site. Is it tidy, clean, safe and well managed? This will give you a sign of the developer's commitment to quality.

▌ Is there a 'Pride in the Job' award-winning mark on site boards? This is another sign that the new homes are being built with quality workmanship.

▌ Before completion check with your solicitor that the property has received its certificate from the NHBC.

▌ Think about getting a home-buyer's or structural survey done.

▌ Check the history of the land use.

▌ If you do have problems within the first two years, put your complaint in writing.

The House Builders Federation promotes new homes and can provide a list of developers working in the area you want to move into. Their website is www.hbf.co.uk or try www.new-homes.co.uk.

Why buy new?

▌ The average new home is up to four times more energy efficient than its Victorian equivalent, and increasingly they use the latest energy-generating technology to make them ever more environmentally friendly.

▌ Maintenance and running costs are almost always lower in a new home than in a second-hand home.

▌ New homes have a ten-year warranty. Warranty providers in the UK include the NHBC and Zurich.

▌ Contemporary designs, a high specification and value for money all come as standard in a new home.

▌ Buying a new home helps avoid the problem of being stuck in a chain. And a part exchange deal is sometimes available to eliminate the expense and hassle of selling through an estate agent.

▌ A new home provides a clean canvas – on which you can stamp your own identity and style in terms of decoration, fixtures and fittings.

▌ Buying a new home means that everything is brand new; you can start living straight away and don't need to spend money or time on redecorating and repairing your home.

Peace of mind

Unlike older homes, new homes come with a comprehensive 10-year warranty to offer you complete peace of mind. Most new houses are protected by NHBC's (National House-Building Council) 10-year Buildmark warranty and insurance. The Buildmark currently covers around 1.6 million properties and provides the most comprehensive protection for new homes in the UK. Established over 65 years ago as a non-profit distributing company, NHBC's primary purpose is to help raise standards in home-construction and improve the quality of new homes. NHBC registers house builders, sets standards of construction, inspects homes and provides consumer protection through its Buildmark Cover. Other warranty providers do exist and your housebuilder will be able to provide you with full details of the warranty they provide.

Buying eco-friendly

House buyers may soon benefit from tax breaks and cheaper properties under a deal to promote 'green homes' being considered by the Government. Ministers are examining proposals that one million UK homes be classified as 'sustainable' by 2012. In France householders already benefit from up to 15 per cent tax credit for carrying out energy efficiency measures in their homes. More information on this can be found http://finances.ambafrance.org.uk. British Gas have already shown how well cash incentives work: by subsidising the costs of energy efficient condensing boilers the company has seen demand for these more modern appliances increase by 700 per cent over three years. And B&Q saw sales of loft and cavity wall insulation jump by 120 per cent when it offered to pay the VAT on such purchases.

Rebecca Willis, Director of Green Alliance, a leading environmental group, said 'The Government will only meet the green targets it has set itself if it is prepared to make the market work for the environment, not against it. Tax breaks that reward householders willing to do their bit are vital, and green groups are looking to the Chancellor to take action.'

The tax incentives are one route being looked at to persuade developers to create new or renovated eco-friendly homes. These would include innovations like:

▌ reduced running costs through greater energy and water efficiency, and reduced maintenance;

▌ healthy internal environments;

▌ access to local amenities and less dependence on car usage;

▌ what materials and resources are used in construction and routine household activities;

▌ the impact on local wildlife.

Whilst it would be unrealistic to call for a million new sustainable homes in 10 years, thanks to ever-improving technology such as solar panels, more efficient boilers, and energy-efficient timber windows, existing homes can be adapted to decent environmental standards at relatively modest cost. The government's Building Research Establishment has been working with conservationists and developers, and has developed an inspection and rating system for new and renovated homes.

'Eco-friendly' on estate agents' details usually means large and expensive, but more modestly-priced properties are now embracing green features. High-level insulation, triple-glazed windows with low-emission glass, and ventilation using recycled 'hot air' are being fitted as standard to many new homes.

You can even give listed buildings a green make-over. A Grade II-listed, four-storey Georgian terraced house in Bath was recently turned into five environmentally-friendly flats. Sash windows were fitted with concealed draught proofing, the roof insulated with lambswool, leaded windows were adapted to provide ventilation to areas with condensation, and piping buried beneath stone flags was lagged with polystyrene. It shows what can be done even with listed buildings. Projects like this transform the image of eco-friendly properties. Perhaps building new homes will not cost the Earth after all.

DIY environmentally friendly tips

▋ Over 40 per cent of all the heat lost in an average home is through the loft and walls;

▋ 250 mm of loft insulation can save up to 25 per cent of your heating costs;

▋ cavity wall insulation can reduce heat loss by up to 60 per cent and can save homeowners up to £100 on their annual energy bills;

▋ double-glazing cuts heat loss through windows by 50 per cent as well as reducing noise and condensation problems;

▋ the older your boiler the more inefficient it will be. If it is 15 years old or more it should really be replaced;

▋ condensing boilers are the most energy efficient and will use up to a third less energy;

- upgrading heating controls will improve the efficiency of any central heating system;

- fit thermostats to radiators to control the temperature in each room;

- put a minimum 75mm insulating jacket on your hot water tank to keep water hotter for longer and check your thermostat is set no higher than 60 degrees Celsius;

- use reclaimed wood for shelves and furniture – placing shelves above radiators ensures that heat is deflected into your rooms;

- the toilet is the biggest consumer of water in your home, using a hippo bag or eco-flush will reduce water use. Worthwhile not only for the financial saving but also the interesting conversation with prospective buyers!

Staying put

Perhaps you are already living in the perfect location. And the house was once perfect too – though now it's little small, as your family grows or grandma moves in. In this case, moving isn't always the best option. When you add up the costs of buying and selling – stamp duty usually being the biggest bill – it often makes sense to stay put and build up, out, or even down.

While having the builders in for weeks or even months can be stressful, as can living on a building site, after the money has been spent and the work finished, most homeowners have the satisfaction of the extra space they wanted and an increase in the value of their property.

The best extensions, in terms of adding value, are bigger dining kitchens and family rooms, according to research by one high street estate agent. Extra bedrooms or an en suite bathroom also make the money back.

Another good value extension is the addition of a granny annexe. No matter how small, buyers later on feel they are getting two properties for the price of one and an annexe has the added advantage of being something that could be let out for extra income.

Unfortunately, though, all repairs and refurbishments are subject to the full 17.5 per cent VAT. Those building their own homes from scratch don't have to pay any VAT on materials.

Extending your current property

Here are some guidelines should you decide to extend:

▌ Consult the local planning authority, who will tell you if you need planning permission. If your home is listed or in a conservation area it will be subject to more restrictive planning laws. You may be able to extend your house without need for planning permission under permitted development rights, but you must check. The Department of the Environment publishes a free booklet, *Planning Permission – A Guide for Householders,* available at council offices.

▌ Look at extensions and conversions at neighbours' homes and ask for recommendations and the numbers of the people who carried out the work. Get several quotes from different architects, surveyors or builders.

▌ Once you have the plans, approach several reputable building firms (if your surveyor/architect is not doing this for you), get estimates and choose one. All building work must meet building regulations and standards and is monitored by the local planning department. The quality of the building work will be examined as will health and safety, services and fire precautions. The Building Controls Officer can demand extra foundations, more drainage, heavier beams, etc, and his requirements will have to be complied with.

▌ How are you going to finance the project? Do you need a loan or a further advance on your mortgage? When calculating costs include the construction expense, new fittings and furnishings and any temporary accommodation. Always overestimate. Check if you are eligible for any home improvement grants.

▌ Plan how long the work will take. Tie the architect/surveyor/ builder down to a contract that includes full details of price and a guarantee as to when the work will start and finish. See if you can include a clause that means they lose money if the work is not finished by a certain date.

▌ Can you live on site? Do you have to? Most builders will move along faster without you on site, but regular visits to monitor progress are a must.

▌ Make sure you have all the correct letters of authority and guarantees for any work you have carried out. They may be necessary when you come to sell. And even if you don't plan on doing the work, it can sometimes add value to your property if you have already obtained planning permission for a conversion or alteration.

Working with your builder

Improving your home doesn't have to result in contractor chaos. Follow these simple guidelines and get the best from your builder.

Check them out

Do your research. Ask the builder about his or her other customers – a good professional will be happy to provide you with references. If they are a member of a trade association, check the membership criteria – and make sure they really are a member. Rogue builders have been known to falsely claim membership. Use the Federation of Master Builder's Find A Builder service.

Get a quote

You need several detailed written quotes and not just 'It'll cost around £300'. A good builder would prefer this anyway; it gives them time to really think about the job and what it will entail.

Draw up a contract

Draw up a written contract with an agreed timetable that both you and the builder are happy with. The FMB has standard contracts for use by anyone using its recommended builders in 'Crystal Mark approved' plain English!

Keep them in the know

Help your builder to understand the look you are going for. Show them magazine pictures of similar projects.

Talk plain English!

Make sure you fully understand every step and don't let jargon put you off. A professional builder should explain things clearly to ensure that there are no nasty surprises! If you're unhappy about the work, talk to your builder immediately. Most things can be amended before they are finished.

Monitoring the job

Keep tabs on how the job is going, particularly if it's a complex project. Arrange a regular half-hour meeting with your builder on agreed days.

It's your home

If you have personal requirements, such as no radios or smoking, or you'd rather not share your lavatory or kitchen facilities, make sure that these are known before the job begins, and provide alternatives.

Always discuss how the builder's rubble will be disposed of, and when.

Dealing with problems

If you do encounter difficulties mid-build:

Be realistic
Builders aren't mind readers, if your project is not going to plan you must spell it out and explain what you *do* want.

Talk to the Boss
Telling sub-contractors to change things mid-construction will not only cause problems within the team but also confuse everyone as to what it is you really want.

Contact the FMB
If you still can't resolve matters with your builder and they are an FMB member, the FMB service includes advising customers and working with both parties to reach a solution.

If you're looking for a vetted builder visit www.findabuilder.co.uk or call 08000 152522.

3 What can I afford?

Many buyers tend to think that what they can borrow and what they can afford are one and the same thing. They aren't.

Work out your budget

Your lender may be willing to lend you a vast amount of money, but the real question is: could you afford to pay it back every month, no matter what happens to interest rates? And have you taken into account the additional costs involved in owning a property?

The best way to work out what you can afford is to add up all the costs associated with home ownership. They break down into two basic components: one-off costs involved in buying the home itself and the ongoing costs of looking after it.

How the costs stack up

Solicitor's fees

If you are buying for the first time or remortgaging your current property, you will have to pay for a solicitor. Some mortgage deals offer to pay your legal costs, up to a certain limit. You will also have to pay the lender's costs involved in the mortgage process. Solicitors and Licensed Conveyancers can charge what they like. Their governing body, the Law Society, says fees should be 'fair and reasonable', based on factors like how much the property is worth, how much work, skill or time is necessary, the place and the circumstance of the conveyancing, whether the land is registered or unregistered, and how important the transaction is to the client.

Do get quotes from more than one conveyancer. The combined cost, including local authority searches, other payments, cash transfers and VAT can add up to more than £1,000 for an expensive home purchase, less outside London or for simpler transactions. Buying and selling at the same time may cost more.

Stamp duty

Stamp duty is a tax on already taxed income levied by the Inland Revenue on property purchases. It's also known as a tax on mobility and can cost you thousands of pounds just to change your address. It has to be paid when you complete your purchase.

For a property costing up to £60,000, there is no stamp duty. Once the price goes above £60,000, stamp duty is charged at one per cent up to £250,000, three per cent between £250,000 and £500,000 and four per cent thereafter. The charge is payable on the full purchase price. For example, a £700,000 house would involve stamp duty of £28,000.

From 1 December 2003, anyone buying a home has had to tell the Inland Revenue when the sale has been completed. They also had to complete a self-assessment of the tax due and pay it within 30 days. The move was part of a crackdown on people who pay less than the market rate for a property, but then pay the vendor an inflated price for 'fixtures and fittings' such as carpets and curtains, in order to stay within a lower tax band.

As I've already mentioned, there are three bands for stamp duty – 1 per cent for properties between £60,000 to £250,000, rising to 3 per cent for homes valued at £250,000 to £500,00, and 4 per cent for property worth more than £500,000. The Inland Revenue is expected to focus on sales of properties very close to the threshold of the tax bands.

So does this rule out paying anything for fixtures and fittings? Not necessarily. You will still be able to pay a vendor money for fixtures and fittings. However, if you are paying an amount that enables you to keep the property price within a certain threshold, you need to accept that the taxman may check up on you. It has always been important to be accurate and tell the truth, but from now on homebuyers will need to be even more careful. Fundamentally there is no difference, in that you can still pay money for fixtures and fittings, providing the valuation is genuine. But homebuyers need to be aware the Inland Revenue have nine months after a sale has been completed to carry out an investigation. The taxman will pay particular attention to cases where the amount paid for fixtures and fittings is 5 per cent or more of the overall value of the property.

Although this may sound high, it will not prevent the taxman from probing purchases close to the stamp duty threshold. Because buyers will now have to fill in an eight-page tax return on completion, the figures are more evident. For homebuyers paying money for fixtures and fittings as part of the sale, this is my advice: be careful, be realistic and keep a clear record of what you paid so you can demonstrate it was a genuine reflection of their worth.

New regulations

It is already more difficult to sell a property valued at £250,000 and £500,000 because of the jump in stamp duty so many buyers and sellers took advantage of a loophole in the rules. This allowed them to do a deal in which the price was set just below the stamp duty threshold, say £249,000, with the buyer paying a separate price for fixtures and fittings, which were not liable for stamp duty. Fixtures and fittings prices of £9,000 were common, so that many £258,000 homes were sold with an under-£250,000 stamp duty rating, saving more than £5,000 in tax.

Now the Inland Revenue has wised up. It was never clear who was liable for stamp duty, but the new legislation – which came into force 1 December 2003 – rules that it is the buyer who pays, giving the taxman someone to pursue. Tax officials will still allow a realistic charge for fixtures and fittings, but have cracked down on anyone who agrees to an inflated price to avoid stamp duty, which will be classed as tax evasion.

Now sellers are likely to get a quicker sale, at a higher price, if they offer to pay some of the stamp duty the buyer will be liable for. So, if they are selling a house at, say, £265,000, they could offer to contribute £5,450 towards the buyer's three per cent stamp duty (of £7,950), rather than drop the price to £249,900. The seller will this way net more – £259,550 – while the buyer will pay only £2,500 in tax.

Estate agent fees

If you have sold your home through an estate agent you will be expected to pay his fee on completion. This can vary from one to three per cent of the price (plus VAT). If you have sold, or are planning to sell, your property yourself, you will also have to factor in advertising rates.

Land Registry fees

These are payable – like stamp duty – on a scale related to the purchase price of the property.

Price of house	Land Registry fee
£0–£40,000	£40
£40,001–£70,000	£70
£70,001–£100,000	£100
£100,001–£200,000	£200
£200,001–£500,000	£300
£500,001–£1,000,000	£500
£1,000,001–£5,000,000	£800

Local authority searches

These are fees payable to local authorities and councils for information about any kind of construction in the area you want to buy a house. Your solicitor has to carry out these searches to find out, for example, if a new by-pass is planned at the bottom of the property's garden, or if planning permission has been granted for a housing estate nearby. The average cost is £65.

There are other searches and payments – company searches, land charges and bank transfer fees, to name but a few – which may have to be budgeted for too. Allow £75 for these to cover the average house purchase.

Home Information Packs

The biggest problem facing a prospective purchaser is that a lot of the crucial information needed to help them make a decision to buy is available only after the offer has been made.

Home Information Packs, which are set to become compulsory in 2006, will contain title documents, replies to standard enquiries, copies of all planning, listed building and building regulation approvals and consents, a draft contract, local authority searches and a home condition report. They are expected to cost an average of £700 and they will have to be compiled by the seller before they even market their property.

The property buying and selling system in England and Wales is one of the slowest in Europe and the introduction of HIPs is meant to speed up the process and cut the cost of delays and failures.

While it's easy to see how first-time buyers will benefit – they will not have to pay to put one together themselves as they aren't selling – there are a few potential problems:

▌ Will all mortgage lenders and buyers be satisfied with a survey organized by the seller?

▌ Some surveys may not be as thorough as demanded and another will have to be paid for.

▌ Where are the 8,000 new Home Condition Inspectors going to come from?

▌ The up-front cost of the HIPs may make some people reluctant sell.

Mortgage redemption charge

If you are moving and therefore repaying the original mortgage, there may be what the lender calls a Mortgage Redemption charge. This is usually calculated on a scale of how long you have had the mortgage. It could be up to three months interest. Check your contract. The lender may try to collect an 'administration' fee too.

Surveys

A surveyor's report on the general state of the property is a prerequisite for lenders and most will not offer mortgages without one. Most banks and building societies offer a choice of three different types of survey – a valuation, a house-buyer's report or a full structural survey.

A structural survey will cost between £300 and £1,200 (plus VAT). There could also be additional costs for drainage checks or an inspection by a CORGI-registered heating engineer.

The house-buyer's report is less detailed and the fee, usually connected to the price of the property, would be between £250 and £350 for a £100,000 home.

The valuation is even less detailed and basically lets the lender know whether or not the property is worth the money you have offered. The cost depends on the value of the property and for under £100,000 would be around £200 but is occasionally carried out free by the lender as part of the mortgage package.

Application fees

Many lenders charge application fees of between £200 and £400 per mortgage application. Some charge even more. Watch out –

sometimes this money is payable even when the application fails or is withdrawn.

Service charges

Before you buy a flat, or even a new house on a prestigious development, check the annual service charge. This is usually the annual cost of maintenance, repair, redecoration and insurance shared between owners. But service charges vary widely. Two apartment blocks may be part of the same residential complex, built at the same time, and look identical – except that the annual service charge for one is thousands of pounds greater than for the other. Always find out first what you are letting yourself in for.

Moving expenses

There is no greater misery than moving home yourself. It doesn't matter how much preparation and planning you have done, it's incredibly hard and time-consuming work. Sometimes there's no choice but to hire a van and get on with it, perhaps with the help of some willing friends and family. But if you can budget for the cost of using a professional removal firm, it is money well spent.

Always get several different quotations and ask for a breakdown of their services. Will they wrap and pack, or do they just collect and drop? And check they are insured.

If you have to do it yourself, you have to factor in the cost of the van (it varies with the size needed), petrol, packing boxes or crates and insurance.

The British Association of Removers offers a few golden rules and handy hints to help you to plan well so that you and your family enjoy the adventure to the full.

■ Choose a company with experience, expertise and facilities to handle your move properly. BAR has a list of recommended members.

▮ Plan your move well in advance. Contact your local moving company up to one month before you hope to move even if you don't know exactly when the big day will be. They will tell you exactly what they will do for you and what you must do yourself. This way you can plan your time and concentrate on the essentials.

▮ Don't move on Friday if you can avoid it. Fridays are always busy and some moving companies will offer a discount if you move in the middle of the week.

▮ Don't do the packing yourself if you can afford to have it done professionally. Packing is not expensive. A good removal company will have the right materials and trained staff who will pack your things much quicker and more safely than you ever thought possible.

▮ Only professionally packed goods will be covered fully by the insurance your remover arranges for you.

▮ Take out insurance. It's not expensive and no matter how much care is taken with packing and handling, moving can be a hazardous business and accidents do sometimes happen.

▮ If you are doing the packing, give yourself plenty of time, it always takes much longer than you think.

▮ Decide what you want to take early and make sure your mover knows when he provides the quotation.

▮ Do not put everything together in one room or area this makes it very difficult for the movers to work and will slow them down.

▮ Remove anything that is not to go to your new home before moving day. If you can't, then identify such items clearly.

▮ If you have something unusual to take with you, let the moving company know. They will make special arrangements for plants, fine art, antiques, wine collections, IT equipment, or anything about which you are particularly concerned.

▌ Keep your mover informed if you think he might need to react at short notice.

▌ Make arrangements with your gas/electricity companies well in advance. Also tell your telephone company and Internet Service Provider and make arrangements to keep your old numbers if possible.

▌ Freezers should be emptied and turned off for long distance moves. For short trips they will be loaded last and unloaded first. However it's best to run down food stocks as much as possible as your mover is not responsible for the contents.

▌ Your mover will take down curtains and lift carpets by special arrangement but will not fit them again in your new home.

▌ Remove light fittings before moving day as your mover is not qualified to do so.

▌ Discuss with your mover whether your furniture is best moved assembled or dismantled. If it's to be dismantled make sure you know whether you have to do it yourself or not.

▌ Leave the contents inside drawers but do not lock them.

▌ Tell your mover if there are parking restrictions at either house. Your mover will make arrangements with the authorities for permission to park if necessary.

▌ Are there any access difficulties at your new home? These will include, narrow streets, overhanging trees, small doorways.

▌ Say if you are moving to a flat or a multi-storey building and whether there is a lift and how big it is.

▌ If necessary you will have to make arrangements for priority use of the lift for the day.

▌ Give the driver clear directions to your new home.

▌ Draw a floor plan of your new home and give it to the foreman so that everything can be put in the correct room.

▌ Try to have small children and pets looked after while the move is taking place. Older children will enjoy the excitement of the move, and should be included as much as possible, to help them understand the reasons for moving and reduce homesickness.

▌ The British Association of Removers, 3 Churchill Court, 58 Station Road, North Harrow, HA2 7SA; telephone 020 8861 3331; or take a look at the BAR website on: www.bar.co.uk

Services

There are a number of service charges to bear in mind:

▌ Electricity – there may be charges for tests or for installing new circuits or additional equipment in your new home.

▌ Gas – check if there are any disconnection or reconnection fees.

▌ Redirection of post – for each surname it costs £6.30 for one month, £13.65 for three months, £21 for six months and £31.50 for one year.

▌ Telephone – there is no connection charge if the line is simply swapped between old and new owners, but you will have to pay if the line is disconnected even if only for a few hours.

Ongoing vs one-off costs

All of the above are one-off costs which refer to the fees you are likely to face when buying a home, including moving in and making it habitable. They can range from a few hundred to many thousands of pounds. Ongoing costs refer to regular maintenance and bills, such as power and council tax or repairs.

Maintenance

Maintaining and repairing your own home can be expensive. Insurance – for both buildings and contents – is a necessity and costs each UK homeowner an average of £450 a year. But insurance doesn't cover everything and it is very easy to spend hundreds of pounds fixing a leaky roof or ancient boiler.

The best way to deal with the unexpected is to set up a contingency fund to help cushion the blow of any large repair or replacement bills.

Garden

If you are busy or simply not green-fingered, it would be a good idea to check the hourly rates of local gardeners. For about £6.50 an hour (more in central London), many will mow the lawn and keep the weeds down. A smart garden increases the value and appeal of a property; an unkempt and overgrown patch is an eyesore and would not make you very popular with the neighbours.

And if it all goes terribly wrong

Help from the State

Help with mortgage payments is available through the benefits system, but is limited:

▌ Income Support for Mortgage Interest (ISMI) will only be paid on a mortgage up to £100,000.

▌ Anyone taking out a loan after 1 October 1995 will not receive ISMI for the first nine months of a claim.

▌ Anyone whose loan was taken out before 2 October 1995 will not receive any support during the first two months of a claim and, during the following four months, only 50 per cent of the eligible mortgage interest will be paid.

▌ ISMI is paid by the DSS at a 'standard rate'. This may not match the rate charged by the lender on the borrower's mortgage account, which could lead to arrears. The Council of Mortgage Lenders has asked the Government to review how the standard rate is calculated to ensure that it is representative of rates charged across all lenders.

▌ ISMI will only pay the mortgage interest and not other outgoings, such as insurance premiums or a savings plan linked to a mortgage. In April 2001, the Government introduced two work incentive measures for homeowners receiving ISMI, namely 'mortgage interest run on' and a new '52-week linking rule'. Under mortgage interest run on, if borrowers come off benefit, they will continue to receive ISMI for a further four weeks. This is aimed at helping claimants back into work. The 52-week linking rule allows claimants to undertake short-term work without then having to wait a further nine months before being able to receive ISMI again.

Help from lenders for borrowers in difficulties

Most lenders will consider cases of financial difficulty and mortgage arrears sympathetically. The first step is to contact the mortgage company to discuss the matter.

With the borrower's co-operation, the lender will develop a plan for dealing with the financial difficulties and clearing the arrears. Most lenders seek to repossess a property only as a last resort.

What happens to a mortgage debt after a home is repossessed?

After a lender takes back a property, interest will generally continue to be charged on the mortgage loan until it is sold. There will also be other costs charged to the mortgage account, including estate agents' costs in selling the property and legal costs.

The lender has a legal duty to sell the property for the best price. If this results in a surplus after all the money owed to the lender and any other secured lender has been repaid, then this surplus is returned to the former borrower. But if the sale proceeds are not enough to pay off the money owing to the lender, the borrower faces a 'shortfall debt', which they still owe to the lender after possession.

What will the lender do if there is a shortfall debt?

The action taken depends on the circumstances. Usually, the lender will contact the borrower as soon as possible after the sale of the property and give a final financial statement. This will show the level of debt still owing to the lender.

If there is a shortfall debt, the lender may:

▌ immediately discuss proposals with the borrower on how they might repay the debt; or

▌ try to give the borrower some time to get back on their feet financially before contacting them about repaying the debt.

How long after the repossession can lenders seek the recovery of the debt?

In England, Wales and Northern Ireland, a lender legally has 12 years in which to contact the borrower to begin the process of obtaining repayment of shortfall debt; this period is usually five years in Scotland.

However, most lenders are committed to fair and sympathetic treatment of people who have suffered repossession and accept that individuals should not face long delays before lenders contact them to discuss repayment of the shortfall. Where a forwarding address is known, most lenders will contact borrowers fairly soon after possession, with a view to agreeing a manageable arrangement for repaying all or some of the debt.

In addition, from 11 February 2000, lenders who are members of the Council of Mortgage Lenders agreed that they will begin all recovery action for the shortfall within the first six years following the sale of a property in possession. Anyone whose property was taken into possession and sold more than six years ago, and who has not been contacted by their lender about recovering any outstanding debt will not now be asked to pay the shortfall.

Does this time limit apply to every case?

The new time limit does *not* affect anyone who is already:

▌ adhering to alternative payment arrangements for the shortfall debt; or

▌ who has already been contacted by the lender, even if the initial contact was made with them by the lender after six years from the date of the sale of the property in possession.

The six-year limit only refers to *beginning* recovery action and does not affect a lender's ability to recover the shortfall debt over a longer period. If there is evidence of mortgage fraud, the new time limit will not apply.

Following the sale of a property in possession, lenders often find it difficult to contact the former borrower. They use a variety of measures to identify where the individual is now living, including using tracing agents. Situations can arise where a lender or its third-party agent is trying to contact the individual (for example, by letter or telephone) to discuss repayment of the shortfall, but the individual simply chooses to *ignore* such contact – despite the fact that the contact is being made at the individual's new address. In these cases, lenders will consider that contact has been made for the purposes of the new six-year limit. If an individual is unclear about whether contact has been made within the six-year period, the lender will be able to confirm the position.

Inheritance tax

Inheritance tax is charged at 40 per cent on estates worth more than £250,000. Latest figures from the Halifax, the country's largest mortgage lender, estimates that the average semi-detached property in London is now worth roughly this amount. The average detached home is nudging £400,000. At this level, inheritance tax would be payable at 40 per cent on the difference between £250,000 and £400,000, which works out at £60,000. Recently, prices in the capital have been increasing at an average of 16 per cent a year, potentially adding more than £25,500 a year to the tax bill. At this rate, inheritance bills for the owner of a detached home in London or the South East could be going up by £500 a week.

Leading financial experts are calling on the Government to reform inheritance tax, arguing that it is unjust. The tax is studiously and easily avoided by the wealthy, and accountants often describe it as a voluntary tax for the rich. Princess Margaret, for example, is thought likely to have given away millions to her children to avoid inheritance tax, even though she still left an estate worth £7.6 million.

The Queen Mother's estate was passed on free of tax through a special concession, although it is thought that she had also put large chunks of money into trust for her grandchildren to ensure that there would be no bills.

But if your main asset is your home, you cannot easily use the devices available to the better off. Tax experts have warned that inheritance tax is a timebomb for homeowners, but appeals to Chancellor Gordon Brown to deal with the issue in his Budget yielded no change.

Inheritance tax, in one form or another, dates back to Roman times but in its modern form it was established in 1894 as estate duty under a Liberal government. The aim was to tax, and redistribute, inherited wealth. In 1975, under Labour Chancellor Dennis Healey, capital transfer tax was set up, with rates at up to a massive 75 per cent on inherited wealth. Capital transfer tax was replaced by the lower inheritance tax under the Conservative government in 1986.

Vulnerable people may be forced to raise mortgages or sell family homes to settle bills. In one case, a widower died, leaving his son, who had been living with him, a £400,000 house. This was the main asset and the son faced an inheritance tax bill of between £60,000 and £80,000. This could only be paid if he took on a mortgage or sold the family home.

One of the most effective ways to reduce inheritance tax liabilities is by gradually giving away assets before death. In families where the main asset is a home, options to reduce liability are limited. Property can pass between husbands and wives free of inheritance tax, so parents could each write wills leaving up to £250,000 to children and the remainder to each other, but this may effectively deprive a spouse of a property or income they need to live on.

Inheritance tax yields about £2.5 billion a year for the Government and to abolish it would cost the equivalent of one penny on income tax. Rather than scrap it, the Government could restructure it. Options include a significant increase in the £250,000 nil-rate band, exempting an individual's home and charging the tax on a sliding scale, rather than the 40 per cent that bites on every £1 over £250,000. Or maybe a capital gains tax on profits from assets at death would be more appropriate. Most homes would escape under rules allowing for a tapered reduction to zero in capital gains tax over a long period.

Many people do manage to avoid inheritance tax, however, either through good planning or through leaving assets to their spouse (which means it is not payable).

Below are some common questions:

What if I leave everything to my husband or wife?
No inheritance tax is payable, but you must both be domiciled in the UK.

What's the inheritance tax threshold?
This is £242,000 and, if you are liable for the tax, it will be levied at 40 per cent. The sum up to £242,000 is known as the nil-rate band.

What deductions are made?
Bequests to a spouse and UK charities are exempt, and outstanding bills, together with funeral costs, will also be deducted from the inheritance tax amount outstanding.

Who pays the tax office?
This will be paid by personal representatives – typically, any children. In some cases, children or heirs can find themselves having to pay the tax bill out of their own funds. Some people find themselves forced to take out bridging loans to meet tax liabilities because they are in the process of disposing of assets, which is why planning before you die can be very helpful.

When is money owed for inheritance tax payable?
It needs to be paid six months after the end of the month when the person has died. The authority to release the money held in the estate is known as probate in England and Wales and confirmation in Scotland.

How can I avoid paying inheritance tax through gifts?
The crucial issue with making gifts to below the inheritance threshold is that they are made seven years before you die – it is, in a sense, a clock ticking when you can beat the tax office.

What are the rules concerning gifts?
Although gifts made in the seven years before your death can be subject to inheritance tax, a number are exempt. A list of these can be found in *An Introduction to Inheritance Tax*, a leaflet available from the Inland Revenue. These gifts include: sums of money of up to £5,000 given as wedding gifts to children; maintenance payments to ex-partners and children; and other gifts of up to £3,000 made during a tax year.

Everyone has this £3,000 limit and, if it's not used up in one year, the amount can be carried forward to the next. After three years, the tax payable on a gift starts reducing until it reaches nil at year seven. Small gifts of up to £250 can be made to any number of people. This is known as taper relief.

The situation concerning gifts can be complicated and, again, it is an area where many people will want to seek advice from an experienced financial adviser.

What are 'potentially exempt transfers'?
It is just another term used for gifts made within the seven-year period to friends and relatives. If you die within the seven years, the value is added to your estate; if you don't, then the gift is exempt. You do not have to tell the tax office about gifts you have made, but the recipient is required to report the gift within a year of the donor's death.

If the death is within three years, 40 per cent is charged; after this, a sliding scale is applied. This is equivalent to a reduction of a fifth if the gift was made between three and four years before your death; another fifth if between four and five years; and so on, until the seventh year.

What are chargeable transfers?
Although there is no inheritance tax charged on a gift made seven years before you die, chargeable transfers can incur tax. These are sums of money transferred typically to trusts for which tax, payable at 20 per cent, is normally levied on the excess above £234,000.

These can also be known as discretionary trusts, which are administered by trustees and where the individual may have no immediate right to income. Gifts to companies are also known as chargeable transfers.

What about giving away a property?
Giving away your home to children or relatives will not mean you are automatically exempt from inheritance tax. If you plan to keep living in it, you need to prove you are paying the new landlord the correct market rent. The landlord could also face a capital gain tax bill when the property is sold, and the inheritance tax sum owed if you die within seven years of making the gift.

What about insurance policies?
Many people have life insurance and if you die and the proceeds are paid into your estate, this money could be subject to inheritance tax if it exceeds the £234,000 limit. The way around this is to have the policy within a trust. Pension fund proceeds passed on to a spouse will also be free of tax.

What about gifts to charity?
Anything left to a UK charity is free of inheritance tax and this also applies to political parties and housing associations.

What about a trust to avoid inheritance tax?
Trusts are a good way of avoiding or paying less inheritance tax and a financial adviser can assist with setting these up. They are not necessarily a total escape from tax though – dependants may still face a tax bill, although at a far lower rate than 20 per cent.

Financial products are held within trusts and are typically provided by insurance companies. It is worth noting that some have higher charges than others. You will need advice on how to set these up. If you do not set up a trust, although you can transfer assets to a spouse tax-free, when they die and pass on wealth to the next generation, inheritance tax will be payable on everything beyond their £234,000 limit.

Life insurance can be written in trust. This applies mainly to whole of life policies. In the case of married couples, for example, a policy would be written on both lives, which pays a death benefit on the second death – when inheritance tax would arise.

You can also buy a policy called a 'gift inter vivos' – meaning a gift between two living people – which is also written within a trust. This is a temporary type of cover, aimed at meeting an inheritance tax liable if you die within seven years of making a lifetime gift. The death benefit will reduce as the potential tax liability reduces.

4 Legal and conveyancing – and buying at auction

Red tape

Conveyancing is the drawing up and checking of the legal contracts and records needed to transfer ownership of property from one person to another.

Typically the process takes about three months, with documentation sent by Royal Mail or Document Exchange, a private postal system used by solicitors. Homebuying in the UK takes twice as long as in most other European countries. According to the Land Registry, the longer conveyancing takes, the more likely the deal is to collapse through 'gazumping', 'gazundering' or the frustration of parties linked in the house-buying chain.

Remember, your solicitor works for you. Unlike the estate agent, whose main responsibility lies with the seller.

The first step is the solicitor acting on behalf of the seller requesting the title deeds – usually from the seller's mortgage company – and copies of the register and title plan from the Land Registry. The solicitor can then draw up the contract, which is sent to the buyer's solicitor, along with any other documents, such as replies to general inquiries.

The buyer's solicitor examines the contract and raises any questions. He conducts searches to ensure there are no plans for building nearby, and there is no contaminated land or old mines that could affect the property. He also checks over any lease. He also receives a copy of the buyer's mortgage offer, usually with instructions to act on behalf of the lender.

CBA LAW FOCUS

We are a niche practice providing property law expertise and in particular with regard to the sale and purchase of freehold and leasehold properties both in the residential and commercial sectors. We also focus on the remortgage market and the buy to let market.

The Firm's Partners are all experienced conveyancers with a range of experience and expertise and they lead a further 12 teams of conveyancers who operate in the carefully risk managed environment utilising the latest technology and providing out of hour services in the evenings and at weekends.

Our Firm has a strong management team who have pioneered a nationwide conveyancing service across England and Wales with a strong emphasis on developing a profile outside the immediate geographical area of the Firm's operation.

CBA Law is the successor to the successful brand name "Moving Direct" and the Firm's initial emphasis was on fixed fees, value for money and the provision of a speedy service.

Our Firm is particularly focused on client need and our Client Relations Department facilitates the provision of out of hours services as well as providing assistance when required to our Fee Earning Unit.

The Firm has plans and ambitions to continue to grow and expand its services with the provision of litigation advice to assist in resolving property disputes as between landlord and tenant, neighbours with boundary disputes and other civil claims.

Contact us for details of our service or for a free quotation on
0800 783 5353 *or visit* **www.cba-law.co.uk**

Once both parties have discussed the searches, answered questions and are satisfied, they sign identical copies of the sale contract, and the buyer's solicitor sends his or her client's contract and deposit to the seller's solicitor. Exchange takes place when the seller's solicitor sends the seller's contract to the buyer.

After this there are more contracts and documents to prepare, mortgage advances and settlement figures requested and transfers to be made before completion, when keys are handed over.

How do I choose my conveyancer?

Recommendation is often a good way to select a service provider such as a conveyancer. Some people prefer to use the family solicitor, while others prefer to go to a licensed conveyancer who deals solely with property matters. Obtaining a few quotes from different solicitors and licensed conveyancers will enable you to compare their prices and services.

You should take several things into consideration when choosing a conveyancer:

█   While cost will obviously be a major factor, you should consider what kind of service you will be paying for. Ask for a breakdown of what the fee includes.

█   Find out when your conveyancer can be contacted and how.

█   Location may also be a factor. If you are relocating out of your area, you will have to decide whether to employ a conveyancer in the area that you are in currently or the area that you are moving to.

How can I speed up the process?

Once you are certain you will be moving and have decided on a conveyancer, there are several things you can do in anticipation of the move that can help to speed up the process.

Your buyer's conveyancer (or your conveyancer for the property if you are buying) will have to undertake searches on the property. If you are selling, your conveyancer may need to get your title deeds to provide a plan of the property, so it is worth getting your conveyancer to request the deeds from your lender or solicitor (if different from the conveyancer) as early as possible.

Depending on the local authority and the amount of work needed to be done, searches can be time-consuming, so the sooner they are made the better.

In the same way as hold ups in any one of these things can cause cumulative delays, dealing with them as early as possible could help to speed up the process.

Your conveyancer may even draw up a draft contract in advance that can be adjusted to fit the details of the specific purchase. This can be done at a very early stage and can also help to avoid delays.

E-conveyancing

The Land Registry, the official body that records who owns what land in England and Wales, believes that by moving the system online, it will become faster and more transparent and reduce the risk of deals falling through. The e-conveyancing system it has proposed will enable authorised solicitors, licensed conveyancers, estate agents, mortgage lenders and other professionals connected with the buying and selling process to conduct business with each other and with the registry using a private, secure, nationwide network. They would have electronic access to the information needed to carry out all stages of the conveyancing process online, including the electronic transfer of money.

In theory, this should enable solicitors to spot and solve problems as soon as they crop up. But the consultation paper asks whether information – not only about their own sale but also about others in their chain – should be made directly available to the public. However, until a majority of the UK population has access to the Internet, solicitors could reasonably argue that communication with clients should still be conducted by post.

The proposed system does not include local councils, and, as anyone who has bought a house knows, obtaining a local search can take many weeks. However, the registry points out that the Government plans to introduce Sellers' Packs by 2006, which means the seller will have to sort out searches before the property is even put on the market.

The new system is not likely to be introduced before 2006. To find out more about the proposals and to have your say about the current system and how you think it can be improved, visit the Land Registry's website (www.landreg.gov.uk).

Do you need to check the title of your property or find out the owners of the house that's been standing empty for years? For just £2 you can find these details online via a new Land Registry service. HM Land Registry for England and Wales is the biggest property database in Europe and, when a property changes hands, registration is compulsory. This will also include leases over seven years, which will bring most commercial properties into the Land Registry net. Property owners will be encouraged to register, as the aim is to have all land registered by 2012.

So will you be able to check the titles of No 10 Downing St, Buckingham Palace or St Paul's Cathedral? Not unless the Crown Estates, the Church Commissioners and the Government volunteer for registration. But on most properties you will be able to find out details of ownership, the price at the last sale, whether there is a mortgage and information on any leases and covenants.

Concerns about privacy and commercial sensitivity have been raised: is this a snooper's charter? Will it increase the vulnerability of those living alone? Unlike the electoral register, the Land Registry shows ownership, not occupancy. However, these details were available on request before the Land Registration Act, which came into force last October 2003. They are just more accessible now.

It will be helpful to many; from the homeowner who is worried that a developer may be buying up houses nearby to the management company of flats tracing absentee lessees. The Act also protects against squatters. Remember the squatter who claimed ownership of a house because he had lived in it for 12 years? In future, the Land Registry must notify the owner if such a claim is made. Provided the owner objects in time, they will be given two years to regain possession. This protection is only for registered property – a strong incentive to apply for voluntary registration.

For more information, log on to www.landregistry.gov.uk.

Auctions

Properties are sold at auctions if they have been repossessed by mortgage lenders, housing associations or councils, or need large-scale work that will deter buyers going through conventional estate agents.

If you are buying, prepare in advance. Most auctions are in hotels and are advertised by participating estate agents and valuers. Contact them for a catalogue of properties under the hammer at the next auction (often this is done via a premium rate telephone line, costing about £5 a call).

The catalogue will contain photos of the properties, details of tenure – mostly 'full vacant possession', meaning no chain – and guide prices, which are normally the minimum the sellers will accept.

If you like the look of a property, visit it well before sale day. Auctioneers arrange group viewings for all potential buyers or ask local estate agents to do individual viewings.

About 15 per cent of properties in catalogues are sold before the auction because a keen buyer has made a deal with the seller, so if you see a property you like in the catalogue, try making an advance bid through the auction house. You have nothing to lose.

Some sellers and their estate agents have 'pre-sale surveys' and will give you details. These are often reliable but most mortgage lenders want an independent survey, and you will have to pay for this – despite running the risk of being outbidded for the property.

Ahead of the auction, arrange a solicitor and mortgage lender as in a conventional house purchase. Ensure you have funds covering the likely sale price (experts suggest the guide price plus 15 per cent to be safe), plus solicitors' fees, moving costs and repair work. You must pay 10 per cent of the property's cost at the auction if your bid is successful.

At the auction each property is called a 'lot'. When your preferred lot comes up, the auctioneer will confirm the address and details before asking for bids. The bids usually rise in £5,000 levels until they approach the guide price, when bids will rise in £2,000 or £1,000 sums. Stay cool and remain well within your budget, or even get a friend to bid on your behalf if you are nervous.

If you are successful, you pay 10 per cent of the cost immediately and the rest within 28 days. Remember – once the hammer has come down, neither the buyer nor the seller can withdraw.

Forthcoming auctions are listed at www.eigroup.co.uk and www.propertyauctions.com.

5 Mortgages

How much can I borrow?

The amount you can borrow depends mainly on your income. You need to find out roughly how much you might be able to borrow before you go house hunting. That way, you know the price range you can afford.

The traditional approach

Lenders generally take the view that buyers can afford about three times their annual pre-tax income, sometimes slightly more. For couples who are both working, the 'income multiple' is generally three times the larger salary, plus one times the second.

Quite a few lenders will be prepared to consider a higher income-to-loan multiple. There are companies out there who offer 100 per cent mortgages and you may find this tempting, but before you opt to borrow more, work out whether you can actually afford it.

Going for a bigger loan

Some lenders will lend on the basis of affordability rather than income multiples. They look at your monthly income and outgoings, and base the amount they are prepared to lend on your individual circumstances. This approach can come up with a much bigger loan than you would normally be offered using

Would you like to...

Spend LESS on your Mortgage
and MORE on Yourself?

Here at Homebank Mortgages Plc, we know how important it is
to make the right decision when it comes to finding the best new
mortgage or remortgage deal. We scan the market for all the
best mortgages out there so that you don't have to.

Select from over **7,000** options

- **Unlock money tied up in your home**
- **Pay off expensive credit cards/loans**
- **Release cash to spend NOW**
- **Find the best deal to suit YOUR circumstances**
- **We cater for every situation including: CCJ's/Arrears**

call TODAY on

0800 052 3604

- **One call –**
to make an appointment with
an advisor local to you for an
independent, professional service

homebank ™

One of The Most Important Decisions You Will Ever Make...

Buying or remortgaging is a financial transaction that is important and needs to be undertaken with care, after all, you want to be able to obtain the best deal that you possibly can.

Homebank Mortgages Plc understands that the vast array of mortgages available – and the choice of different lenders to choose from – can make this crucial decision complex and confusing. This is why they always recommend seeking the advice of a registered mortgage advisor. As independent brokers, they do not work for any one lender (their sole purpose is working to find the best deal for their client), which means that they can use their expertise of the market and lenders – many of which do not have a high street presence – to find the best mortgage rate for each and every individual they work for. They can also deal with more niche lending.

Yet, there can be a reluctance to use a broker because of the fee involved...but what many forget is that not only is time and money saved in sourcing the right product, but the difference in the total cost between the most and least favourable mortgage for the client can be measured in tens of thousands of pounds over the full mortgage term! Some niche lenders only market via brokers, and can offer mortgages to those who don't fit the normal lending criteria – such as those with an adverse credit history, the self-employed and those needing non-standard lending. Another difference is that whilst the high street lender will offer attractive response rates to new customers – as opposed to loyal good paying ones, an independent mortgage adviser will **always** strive to offer you the best rates. Qualified *Cemap/MAQ Registered Mortgage Advisers with **Homebank™** use an exclusive sourcing system that will source from literally thousands of mortgages to find the best deal for each and every client.

The real value of using an independent broker is what they have saved you. By conducting a thorough and comprehensive fact find and really getting to know your circumstances and needs, they are able to conduct their findings on understanding your requirements as well as finding you the best possible deal. This research is always individually done for each and every client, ensuring the best possible deal for different needs and circumstances.

Registered Mortgage Advisers also carry a wealth of knowledge in all types of mortgages, for both experienced property owners and first-time property buyers. **Homebank™** provides a personal and professional service *across the UK* for: *remortgage, purchase, buy-to-let, self-certification, self-build or right-to-buy*, *whatever the individual circumstances*.

Any reputable mortgage broker/adviser will be regulated by the MCCB (Mortgage Code Compliance Board). From 31 October 2004, this will be overtaken by The Financial Services Authority. The responsibility for mortgage regulation will fall on the Financial Services Authority.

For further information and advice on how you could save money on your mortgage call Homebank™ on **0800 052 3604** or visit their website at **www.homebankplc.com**

*Certificate in Mortgage Advice and Practice/Mortgage Advice Qualification

traditional income multiples. Do your budgeting carefully if you take up such an offer.

Keeping your payments down

Generally speaking, you should try not to pay more than 40 per cent of your net (take home) pay in mortgage payments. This is just a guideline: in London, for example, you may well find half your income going on the mortgage.

On top of that there are the ongoing costs of owning a house: council tax, utilities and maintenance. It's hard to estimate costs before you move in, but overall you should try to keep the total cost of your home to a maximum of 60 per cent of your monthly take-home pay.

The valuation limit

Most people borrow only 95 per cent of the property's valuation, which can be lower than the price you have agreed with the seller. Many lenders give better deals to people with large deposits, so it can make sense to dip into savings, as the smaller the deposit, the higher the interest rate you may have to pay.

You can get 100 per cent mortgages, but the rates are generally uncompetitive and you will pay above the odds to borrow at this level. It is much better to save for a deposit.

The size of your mortgage compared to the value of your property is called the loan to value (LTV) ratio – a £90,000 mortgage on a £100,000 home gives a LTV of 90 per cent. The Council of Mortgage Lenders says the average first-time buyer's mortgage is 74 per cent LTV, and their average mortgage is £86,000. Other buyers have an average 62 per cent LTV ratio with a £93,000 mortgage.

Finding the right mortgage for you

Mortgages come in a wide and confusing variety, but if you choose carefully you should be able to get a mortgage that suits you. You need to decide first on the type of loan you want, then think about which approach to repaying your loan is best for you.

The following is a brief summary of the main types of loan available:

■ **Variable rate:** the standard mortgage product, and often the most expensive of the range available. Rates move up and down more or less in line with the Bank of England base rate, but at the lender's discretion and at a level typically 1.75 per cent higher than base rate.

■ **Tracker rate:** the rate is guaranteed to move in line with the Bank of England base rate by a set amount and usually for a set period, although in some cases the guarantee is for the life of the mortgage.

■ **Discounted rate:** you get a discount on the standard variable rate, or the tracker rate, for a set period. This is often set in steps, with the discount decreasing in stages over a year or more.

■ **Fixed rate:** the rate you pay is fixed for a set period, typically between one and five years. Your monthly payments therefore stay the same during that period, regardless of what happens to interest rates. However, beware of any redemption penalties that might tie you in to the lender's variable rate after the fixed period has ended.

■ **Capped rate:** the rate cannot go above a specified upper limit, but will follow rates down if they fall. Like fixed rates, these are normally for a set period, between one and five years.

■ **Cashback:** you get a cash payment when the loan is finalised, generally as a percentage of the loan amount, eg three per cent. You usually have to pay the standard variable rate for a fixed period, or pay back some of the cash if you want to get out of the deal early.

■ **CAT standard:** the loan meets standards laid down by the Government for costs, access and terms. These ensure that you pay a fair rate of interest and there are no hidden charges or unfair terms in the small print.

■ **Flexible:** this is really a repayment option rather than a type of loan. It helps you to pay off your mortgage earlier without penalty and cut your interest costs.

How do you want to repay your mortgage?

It is worth thinking about your mortgage loan even before you hit the high street or search the Internet. There are only two main ways to pay off the mortgage, but they are very different in the way they work and the effect they have on your debt.

Debt is an expensive luxury, especially when inflation is low and there are no tax breaks on debt interest. Aim to pay off your mortgage as quickly as possible – it is the most effective form of saving there is. You can do that by choosing a shorter repayment term than the usual 25 years, for example.

Repayment mortgage

A repayment mortgage is guaranteed to pay off your mortgage by the end of the term. That makes it the safest way to repay your loan. It works just like a normal personal loan – each month, you pay back some of the original capital plus interest on the outstanding balance.

In the early years, most of your repayments are made up of interest, with the result that you only pay off a small proportion of the capital. But you can pay in extra lump sums, or overpay regularly, to reduce your debt and cut the amount of interest you have to pay. Redemption penalties on some special deals may prevent you doing this, though, so check first.

The Mortgage Minefield

Unless you are an experienced property developer or landlord, when you come to buy a home you will be faced with a baffling array of choices. To whom should you turn to get expert, trustworthy advice?

Without appropriate advice, you could be walking into a minefield! Buying a home is a pretty frenzied activity, at the best of times; there are so many issues to think about. In addition, moving home – whether as a first-time buyer or trading up or down, is usually associated with a major change in your life.

With many other issues of concern, prospective home-buyers rarely have the time to find the right mortgage for themselves and would normally visit their bank or building society but this may not be the best solution.

How do you ensure that the advice you get is right for you? Your advisor should supply his Terms of Business and be truly independent. He should use the entire market, not just a limited panel of lenders and not be required to submit a "quota" of cases to specific lenders. Any fees he charges should be reasonable and justified by the quality of his service so he will not be "tempted" to place your mortgage with the lender that pays him the most.

The advice you receive should be in writing, full, clear and understandable. It should spell out the reasons for the mortgage selection, what the benefits are to you, how much it will cost, what charges the lender will make if you decide to pay off the loan early, etc. The intermediary should also declare any fee he will receive from the lender.

Over recent years increasing concerns have been expressed about protecting the public. As a result, a number of changes have taken place within the mortgage industry to improve its quality and the public's perception of it. On 1st November 2004, the Financial Services Authority will take over regulation of the industry, putting it on the same footing as all other financial services.

Most mortgages are paid back over a period of 25 years, but you can opt for a shorter repayment period if you can afford the higher payments. Depending on your age, you may also have to accept a shorter period.

Repayment mortgages are good if you prefer the safety-first approach and want to be sure you will eventually pay off your mortgage.

Interest-only mortgage

If you opt for an interest-only mortgage, your monthly payments will seem much cheaper than those for a comparable repayment loan. But that's because you are only paying back interest – it's up to you to come up with the cash to repay the original loan amount at the end of the mortgage term (usually 20 or 25 years).

Most people decide to set up an investment plan to pay off the capital they owe. This can be stock market-based (using an individual savings account (ISA), for example) or through an endowment policy. These are no longer very popular as they tend to be inflexible and expensive.

All mortgage-linked savings schemes should aim to grow at a rate higher than the amount you are paying in interest. If they fail to achieve this, they will not provide enough money to pay off your mortgage.

A few people don't take out investments but rely on house price rises to pay off their loan when they sell up. This can be risky if you don't have much of a deposit to put down on a property – and if prices drop instead of going up.

You can make capital repayments with an interest only mortgage to reduce your mortgage debt faster and cut interest payments, just as you can with a repayment mortgage. But check there are no redemption penalties first.

Interest-only mortgages are good if:

▋ you expect investment returns (after charges) to be higher than mortgage rates;

▌ you expect to earn bonuses that you can use to pay down your mortgage regularly, or inherit money that you can use to pay off your mortgage;

▌ you expect house prices to rise substantially so that you have enough equity in your property to pay off your loan.

They are not so good if you don't want to take the risk that your investment will not grow fast enough to pay off the mortgage.

Flexible and current account/offset mortgages

Flexible mortgages are repayment mortgages that enable you to pay off your mortgage earlier and cut your interest costs. They offer the ability to overpay, underpay, and take payment holidays. Any overpayments you make are immediately credited against what you owe. With traditional mortgages, overpayments are usually only credited once a year, and may not be possible at all if redemption penalties apply.

Flexible mortgages also charge interest on a daily or monthly basis, instead of the normal annual basis. This makes a big difference to the amount of interest you pay in total.

Most flexible loans are traditional mortgages with additional flexibility. These come in the usual variety, with discounted, fixed and tracker rates available.

Truly flexible loans are the relatively new type of current account or offset mortgage products. Both types allow you to put your mortgage, credit card, personal loan, current account and savings in one pot. This effectively means you earn tax-free interest on your savings as all your money is being used to offset your mortgage. And all your borrowing is also effectively at a lower rate of interest.

The main difference between the two types of account is that the current account product puts everything in one pot, producing one statement, while offset products keep your accounts separate.

Flexible loans are good if:

▌ you expect to be able to make overpayments, either regularly or occasionally;

▌ you have irregular earnings that make flexibility with mortgage payments important;

▌ you can benefit from the tax and interest advantages of having all your money in one pot. This generally applies to high earners and people with significant savings to offset their debts.

Flexible loans are not good if:

▌ you are unlikely to use the flexibility, need to budget or want to keep your mortgage costs as low as possible. Flexible loan rates are not usually the most competitive, and you may be better off with a discounted or fixed rate mortgage in these circumstances;

▌ you are undisciplined with money. Current account mortgages in particular are no good for spendthrifts who cannot mentally put aside an amount to pay the mortgage each month, when it does not physically disappear from their account.

Pension-linked mortgage

It's unusual to see these being sold today, although you may have a pension-linked mortgage if taken out a few years ago. Basically, you are expected to use the tax-free lump sum from a maturing pension to pay off your mortgage.

The attraction is that all payments into a personal pension attract generous Inland Revenue tax rebates. Review your repayment plan regularly to make sure it is still on track to pay off your mortgage. You may have to increase payments if growth is lower than expected.

Repaying an interest-only loan

At a time of soaring property prices many buyers choose an interest-only mortgage because the monthly repayments are cheaper. Some really live dangerously and put off setting up any investments to pay off the capital at the end of the term. But this isn't advisable unless you are very confident about your future finances.

The main ways people do pay off interest-only loans are outlined here.

ISAs

Saving cash in an individual savings account (ISA) is increasingly popular as a way to back up your mortgage. You'll need to pick up a fund investing in stocks and shares that are expected to grow fairly fast – if the ISAs do well, you could pay off the mortgage early.

You can put up to £7,000 into a stock market ISA each tax year, so a couple can make £14,000 worth of investments. The downside is that you will open yourself up to stock market fluctuations.

Endowments

Endowments are savings schemes with built-in life insurance, sold by insurance companies. The contract usually runs for 25 years, meaning you can't pay off the loan early.

With-profits endowments offer you an annual bonus, which can't be taken away, plus a further bonus when the policy matures. This can be worth up to 60 per cent of a policy's final value. Your cash is invested in a giant fund containing stocks and shares, property and fixed-interest investments.

Endowments have some well-publicised performance problems, so be very cautious if you are offered one. An ISA is easier and cheaper to run than an endowment, and a lot more flexible. Salespeople earn a lot of commission from selling endowments, so some firms still try the hard sell. Watch out.

Long-term fixed-rate mortgages

The Government want to see more long-term fixed-rate home-loans as a way of stabilising the UK property market. Lenders like long-term products because there is a higher likelihood that borrowers will stay with them. And some homeowners like the security of knowing exactly what their mortgage payments are going to be for the next 10, 15 or even 20 years. But there are several things to consider before signing up to a long-term fixed rate loan. Can you get out without paying penalties? Can you overpay? Can you keep the mortgage when you move house and can you borrow more at the lender's best rates? Also ask yourself how you would feel if interest rates fall and you were tied in to a long-term fixed-rate which would not allow to you to change to a cheaper deal?

Euro mortgages

A euro mortgage is the same as a normal mortgage except that the loan is measured in euros rather than in pounds. That's important because the rate is based on the lower euro interest rate rather than the higher UK rate, meaning that you pay less. The problem is that the borrower has to take a risk to get that lower interest rate – the risk lies in the exchange rate. Exchange rate changes can be a disaster if you borrow in one currency to buy something valued in another currency because if the euro strengthens against the pound, your euro loan will get bigger in sterling terms. Although it's unlikely, in theory you could end up owing more than the house is worth so euro mortgages are probably best left to investment professionals and people paid in euros who do not have to run the risk of the exchange rate moving against them.

How to find the best deal

Shop around

Small or obscure building societies and mortgage brokers often offer better rates than High Street banks and building societies.

Mutuality pays

Building societies generally offer a better mortgage deal than most banks, certainly on variable rates. And with some societies, there is the possibility of a demutualisation windfall if the society floats on the stockmarket or is taken over.

Look beyond the headline rate

The initial interest rate quoted in tables or adverts may be temptingly – but also temporarily – low. Find out what rate you will pay when the special deal finishes.

Check for redemption penalties

These are common on many types of mortgage, and make it expensive to switch out of a loan while they apply. They usually apply only for the term of a special deal, but they may extend beyond that term where the initial rate is particularly low, tying you into the lender's standard variable rate for several years. Loans like this with extended penalties are not usually good value.

Watch out for compulsory insurance

To qualify for some loans, you have to buy insurance from or through your lender – typically buildings or contents cover. You can invariably buy such cover more cheaply from another source.

If you are considering such a deal, factor in additional interest of at least 0.25 per cent to reflect the price of an uncompetitive insurance policy.

Will you have to pay a MIG?

If you are borrowing more than 90 per cent of the value of your home you may be asked to pay a mortgage indemnity guarantee (MIG) – sometimes called a 'high lending fee'. This is a one-off payment that buys an insurance policy that will pay out if you get into mortgage arrears and the house is repossessed. But beware – this does nothing to protect you! Many lenders don't charge a MIG any more. If it's demanded from you, check whether you could get a better deal elsewhere.

How often is interest calculated?

Daily or monthly calculations work better than annual ones for borrowers who want to repay capital regularly. With annual interest any capital repayment made over a 12-month period is only credited once a year, on a lender's chosen anniversary. The interest you pay throughout the next 12 months relates to the sum owed at that earlier point. With daily or monthly interest, all capital repayments are credited as soon as they are made. This means that future interest you pay relates to the reduced sum still left outstanding. Because you owe less, you pay less interest.

Check minimum capital repayment to trigger a recalculation

Most lenders who calculate interest annually will do a recalculation if you pay in a big enough lump sum and ask for the calculation to be done. Find out what the minimum is – it may be just £100 or up to £1,000.

Take all costs into account

When comparing mortgage costs, be sure to include application, valuation, legal and other fees. If the rate varies over the term of any special deal, work out what rate you will pay on average and use that in comparisons.

Beware the stated APR (annual percentage rate)

Depending on many hidden factors, a loan with a low APR may be more expensive overall than one with a higher APR.

Getting advice

Advice on mortgages is offered by estate agents, mortgage brokers, financial advisers, and lenders – but there are no laws governing mortgage advice, so tread carefully.

What sort of advice will you get?

Lenders will only offer advice on their own products. Estate agents will generally deal with a few lenders with which they have a relationship. Some estate agents are subsidiaries of a lender, and only offer mortgages from that lender. If you want advice, mortgage brokers are a better bet, although they, too, may deal with a panel of lenders rather than covering the whole market.

If you use a mortgage broker, find out how you will be charged before you start discussions. Some brokers get paid entirely by commission from lenders, while others charge a fee, typically one per cent of the loan you take.

Follow the mortgage code

There are no laws governing quality or training standards for mortgage advisers, as there are for investment advisers. But most lenders and mortgage intermediaries follow a voluntary code of conduct, which includes guidelines for giving advice. The code says that brokers must tell you:

■   whether they trawl the whole marketplace to find the most suitable mortgage or choose from a panel of selected lenders;

■   whether they are acting as your representative or the lender's;

■   whether they will receive a fee from the lender for putting mortgage business their way.

You can find out whether a mortgage broker subscribes to the mortgage code by asking for their registration number. Or check with the Mortgage Code Compliance Board to see if they are registered on the helpline number 01785 218200.

Can you save yourself money by remortgaging?

Remortgaging is what you do when you switch your mortgage to a new lender without actually buying a new home.

Why remortgage?

Like millions of borrowers, you probably have a variable rate mortgage. If you don't have a redemption penalty on your current loan, you could save many hundreds of pounds a year by switching to a better value fixed or discounted loan. For example, if you are paying 7.5 per cent on a standard variable rate, your monthly interest payments on a £100,000 interest-only loan work out at £625. Switch to a discounted rate where you pay 5.5 per cent for one year and your monthly payments immediately fall to £458, a saving of £2,000 over a year.

With savings like these to be made, it may be worth switching your loan even if you would have to pay a redemption penalty.

You need to work out how much you will save compared with the penalty involved.

Are there any costs?

You may have to pay an application fee, a valuation fee and solicitors' fees too. That could add up to £700 or £800, which may wipe out any potential savings from a lower rate if you have a small loan.

Some lenders offer special deals for borrowers looking to remortgage to minimise these costs. The rate may not be the most competitive, but it is balanced by benefits such as a free valuation, no application fee, and cashback of £250 or £300 to cover your legal costs. This can work well if you have a small loan.

It is worth talking to your own lender before moving your mortgage to find out if they can offer you a better deal. You could avoid some of the costs involved in switching to a new lender.

Research the market

Take a good look around before deciding where to apply. You may get special remortgage terms from some lenders, but you will also be excluded from some deals that lenders do not make available to borrowers who want to remortgage. These are some of the points to watch:

- Look at the rate you will move on to after any special deal has ended, and think about whether it might mean having to remortgage again in a few years' time.

- Consider, instead, switching to a lender who offers good value over the longer term, perhaps by pledging to maintain a competitive standard variable rate.

- Take a look at flexible current account and offset mortgages to see if they would suit you. The tax advantages and cost efficiency of such schemes can be compelling.

Take a look at the earlier section on How to Find the Best Deal (see pages 73–75) to brush up on the pitfalls of the mortgage market.

Getting a mortgage if you are self-employed, work on contract or have an impaired credit record can be hard work. But now competition between lenders is so intense most obstacles can be overcome.

Hard-to-get mortgages

Self-employed

If you haven't been self-employed for very long, you will probably find it hard to get a loan until you have established yourself, unless you have gone into a business in which you are already experienced and can demonstrate a track record.

Lenders will generally want to see three years of accounts to prove your income before deciding whether to offer you a loan. But they are gradually getting more relaxed about this sector of the economy, and some lenders are happy with 12 months of accounts.

One common problem if you are self-employed is that your accounts are likely to understate the profits from your business, for perfectly legitimate reasons. That cuts down the amount you can borrow. One way around this is to opt for a self-certification loan, where you state what your income is, but do not have to prove it. This type of loan is generally more expensive than conventional loans, and has the added drawback that you may not be able to borrow as large a proportion of the property's value.

Contract workers

Contract workers may have to shop around to find a lender willing to take them on, or use a mortgage broker who will know which lenders to approach. Some lenders will want to see that your contract has been renewed regularly over a one or two year period. Others may be happy if your contract has been renewed at least once by the same employer.

Mortgage arrears

You may be turned down for a mortgage if you have fallen behind with your payments on a previous loan. Lenders conduct a credit search to discover your credit history, and often use a system of credit scoring to assess your creditworthiness. If you don't get enough points, you could be refused a loan, and mortgage arrears will obviously affect your score.

Many lenders will lend to people with a history of mortgage arrears, but only under certain conditions. They may limit the proportion of the property value they are prepared to lend, and specify a maximum number of months' arrears, typically three or six months. They may also refuse to consider your application if the arrears occurred within a specified time period, for example, within the last 12 months.

You may have to turn to specialist lenders if you cannot meet the conditions demanded by mainstream lenders. But that will generally mean having to pay a higher rate of interest. You can take a look at the conditions specified by lenders if you select the 'arrears' category of mortgages in the mortgage tables and click through to each lender's details.

County court judgements

County court judgements, or CCJs, are issued for unpaid debt. They stay on your credit reference file for six years from the date of the judgement, or until the debt is paid off.

If you cleared the debt more than a year ago, you stand a good chance of getting a mortgage from mainstream lenders. You are likely to find it harder if you paid it off more recently; and if it is still unpaid, you will generally be refused a mortgage by High Street lenders. Specialist lenders may offer you a loan, but on uncompetitive terms.

You can take a look at the conditions specified by lenders for CCJs if you select the CCJs category of mortgages in the mortgage tables and click through to each lenders' details.

Checking your credit history

If you want to check your own credit rating, send your name and address, together with a cheque or postal order for £2 and a list of your previous addresses over the last six years, to both of the following agencies:

Equifax
Credit File Advice Centre,
PO Box 3001,
Glasgow, G81 2DT.

Experian
Consumer Help Service,
PO Box 8000,
Nottingham, NG1 5GX.

First-time buyers

Getting 100 per cent

Several lenders offer 100 per cent mortgages, although not all make them available to first-time buyers. Scottish Widows even offer 110 per cent on its Professional Mortgage – a loan aimed at those in structured careers, who are likely to earn more as they get older.

There are a couple of problems with 100 per cent loans. First, there is the potential for negative equity. If the value of your property falls by 5 per cent and you have a 10 per cent stake in it, you still have 5 per cent equity in the property. If it falls by 5 per cent and you don't have equity in the property, you are in a negative equity position.

Few economists believe house prices will fall in the near future, but some lenders like the NatWest and Alliance & Leicester have decided to restrict 100 per cent deals in some areas.

Another problem with 100 per cent deals is they tend to attract higher rates than smaller mortgages. For instance, a borrower who puts down a 10 per cent deposit is only charged 5.99 per cent for two years (by one supermarket lender) but those who take a 100 per cent loan are charged 6.3 per cent. However, once you have built up 10 per cent equity in the property you can move to the lower rate.

Any cashback?

An alternative to a 100 per cent mortgage is a cashback deal. At Bristol & West you may be denied 100 per cent as a first-time buyer but you can borrow 95 per cent loan-to-value (LTV) and get 5 per cent cashback to spend as you choose. Some lenders offer much more than this.

Cashback is useful but often comes with redemption penalties. Most lenders will ask you to repay the money if you redeem in the early years so you may be better off just using your credit card for extra cash – especially if you choose one with a good introductory rate.

Firsts for first-timers

The first-time buyer market has seen a couple of innovations recently. The rent-a-room mortgage from the Marketplace at Bradford & Bingley allows you to take potential rental income into account when applying for a loan. For example, if you can get a lodger to pay £80 a week you can add £4,160 to your income, which means you can borrow about £13,520 more.

Another new scheme is Newcastle Building Society's Guarantor Mortgage. The lender takes into account money that can be guaranteed by a parent or relative. If you earn £20,000, Newcastle would typically offer you a mortgage of £80,000, but if the property you want to buy costs £100,000, it will let the £20,000 shortfall be guaranteed. Once you earn enough to take the mortgage on yourself, the guarantor will be relieved of their responsibility. You will still need a large deposit for the scheme – the maximum LTV is 85 per cent – but it could help you get your first home.

Shared ownership schemes

If house prices in your area make it difficult to afford your own home, find out if you can take advantage of a shared ownership scheme. Under this, you raise a mortgage to cover a proportion of the value of the property, and pay subsidised rent on the balance. You can increase your stake in the property after a year, and carry on doing so until you are the full owner.

Shared ownership schemes are run by housing associations and local councils. Most have long waiting lists and may give preference to those already renting council or housing association accommodation.

Each scheme has different criteria, but prospective buyers will generally need a regular income, and be required to complete a means test.

Shared ownership loans are available from around 20 lenders, including several High Street names. Most offer a range of loans, including fixed and discounted rates.

Right to Buy

If you have lived in a council property for two years or more you have a Right to Buy. You can either purchase outright or buy to rent on mortgage terms. That means you buy the property for less than the Right-to-Buy price with money from a lender, which will then charge repayments no more than your current rent. If you buy outright you will qualify for discounts, depending on length of tenancy and type of property. The Government introduced new rules last year (2003), so check with your local council exactly what their requirements are.

Buying a leasehold property – to buy or not to buy the lease?

If you 'buy' a leasehold flat, you don't own the building – you own the right to live there for a specified period of time – however much time remains on the lease. Many leases are granted on a 99-year term while some run for 999 years.

Most banks and building societies are happy to lend on property that has at least 75 years unexpired on the lease.

More than two million people own property on a leasehold basis. If you are one of them and you have the opportunity to purchase the lease, it is almost certainly worth buying. A lease is a depreciating asset and as the years left to run diminish, it will become increasingly difficult to sell.

If you have a flat in a block, you and the other leaseholders can buy the freehold collectively if you meet certain complicated criteria. At least two-thirds of the flats must be owned by tenants whose leases were originally granted for at least 21 years. Of those, at least two-thirds must be in favour of taking on the freehold, and the participating flat owners have to own at least half the flats in a block. Half the participating flat owners must have lived there for a qualifying period, which is one year, or for three out of the last 10. As long as you meet these conditions the landlord has to sell but you will probably need a solicitor and a surveyor to act for you because the law is complex.

If you do not want to buy the freehold you can extend your lease but legal costs could reach the £1,000 to £1,500 mark. To qualify, your lease must have been granted for at least 21 years and you have to satisfy the 'low rent test'. This is a complicated sum based on your flat's rateable value. It is to be abolished for people extending leases longer than 35 years but a date for its removal has yet to be set. You must have lived in your flat for at least three years.

You can get advice on these issues from LEASE, the Government-funded advisory service. LEASE can be contacted at 6 Maddox Street, London W1, telephone: 020 7493 3116.

With all these options, buying your first home may not be quite as hard as you first thought.

6 Insurance

There are various types of insurance you will need to consider when buying a property and taking out a mortgage. This is a summary of the main points to take on board. You are likely to be offered various types of insurance by your lender, but they may not be particularly competitive. It is always worth checking if you can get cheaper cover elsewhere. Some lenders offer insurance cover as part of a mortgage, but this is rarely the best value. Check the terms of your employment before you buy cover. You may not need life cover, for example, if you are covered under your firm's pension scheme.

Buildings insurance

Buildings insurance covers you for damage to your property and any fixtures and fittings that you would not be able to take with you if you moved.

If you are buying a leasehold flat, you don't usually have to worry about taking out buildings insurance. The landlord generally arranges cover, with the cost included in the service charge. In most other cases, buildings insurance is your responsibility. Your lender will insist that you take out cover via them if you do not buy it elsewhere.

The cost of insurance will depend mainly on where you live. Premiums are likely to be higher than average if there is a history of subsidence in your area, or if you live on a flood plain. In the latter case, insurers may exclude damage caused by flooding altogether.

You need to insure for the cost of rebuilding, which is often higher than the market value of your property. The danger of under-insuring is that any claim you make could be scaled back in proportion.

Contents insurance

Contents insurance covers you for damage to the contents of your property. You don't have to buy it, but it makes sense to do so. The cost will depend on where you live, how much cover you want, and the type of cover you choose.

The following are some points to consider:

▌ Check what risks you are covered for. You may have to pay extra to get cover for accidental damage. Choose 'all risks' cover if you want to be insured against loss of, or damage to, valuable items you take out of your home.

▌ Be as accurate as possible about the value of your possessions, and insure for that amount. If you underinsure, you run the risk of a reduced pay-out if you make a claim.

▌ Think twice if the insurer insists on you taking security precautions, such as locking all windows or turning on an alarm. You could have a claim turned down if you don't stick to the agreed conditions.

Mortgage protection insurance

Mortgage protection insurance covers your mortgage payments for a set period if you are unable to pay due to accident, sickness or unemployment. You don't get much help from the State if you have problems paying your mortgage, so it is worth considering taking out insurance, but check carefully that any policy is suitable for your circumstances.

These are the main points to watch for:

I   Self-employed people and short-term contract workers could find it hard to make a claim for unemployment.

I   You will not be able to claim for any time off work due to an illness or disability that existed before you took out the policy.

I   There is always a waiting period of 60 days before your policy will pay out after you make a claim.

I   The policy will usually pay out for up to 12 months when you make a claim. Some insurers offer longer benefit periods.

I   Expect to pay around £5 or £6 per £100 of payments you want to cover.

Life insurance

You need to take out life insurance if it is important that the mortgage will be paid off if you die, essentially if you have dependants.

I   Choose *term assurance*, the cheapest type of life cover, which pays out if you die during the term of the policy, but gives nothing back if you don't.

I   You want *level term cover* if you have an interest-only loan, or you can opt for decreasing term if you have a repayment mortgage.

I   Couples get better value from *buying a policy each*, rather than one that covers them both.

Critical illness cover

Critical illness cover pays out a lump sum if you suffer any of the conditions named under the policy, such as cancer, a heart attack, or a stroke. The younger you are, the less you pay, so it is worth considering taking out a policy to cover your mortgage even if the possibility of claiming seems remote.

Permanent health insurance

Permanent health insurance (PHI) pays a monthly income if you cannot work because of ill health. Unlike mortgage protection insurance, it pays out until you go back to work, or to age 65 if you can't work at all. It is worth having, particularly for the self-employed. But it is expensive, and therefore unlikely to appear on the shopping list for most mortgage borrowers.

Landlord's insurance

If you are buying a property with the intention of letting it, your lender will require extra cover for home and contents, and this can work out around 50 per cent more than normal insurance premiums.

Removals insurance

Reputable removal companies will have their own insurance which covers furniture and equipment they pack – but not damage to items the householder has packed. It's up to you to make sure your policy covers items in transit if you have packed them yourselves. Do check the small print for exclusion causes. If you have a particularly precious or fragile piece of antique furniture or jewellery, or important computer equipment, it may be worth packing them carefully yourself and taking them in your own car.

7 Making the move

Buying a property and moving in is definitely up there on the list of life's most stressful events. So anything you can do to make the process run smoothly is good news. Here are the main steps to follow.

Obtain a mortgage offer in principle

Ideally, this should be done before you start looking for a home. That's because it gives you an idea of how much you can afford. It also establishes you as a more serious home purchaser with estate agents you contact. If you haven't obtained an offer-in-principle yet, do it as soon as possible.

Find a solicitor

The moment you make an offer and it is accepted, you need to tell the estate agent who your solicitor is, so that he or she can pass the details to the vendor's own lawyers. Find a lawyer before you make the offer, or straight after. Always get a quote from several before choosing one. Make sure you are comparing like with like: does the quote include search fees, VAT, phone calls, letters and postage, or bank transfer fees?

<u>Golden Rules to Moving Home</u>

Always choose a BAR member

The British Association of Removers (BAR) is the largest established and recognised Trade Association for removals companies.

All member companies must meet strict standards and are inspected on a regular basis to ensure that their facilities, equipment and expertise remain at the highest level.

In fact, fewer than 700 removals companies in the whole of the UK can claim to be members.

Plan your move well in advance

Contact your local moving company up to one month before you hope to move even if you don't know exactly when the big day will be. They will tell you exactly what they offer and the areas you need to think about. This way you can plan your time and concentrate on the essentials.

Where possible, ask at least three removal companies to visit and quote on your move. Don't necessarily choose the cheapest, and be aware that the most expensive doesn't mean that this will be the most proficient.

Don't do the packing yourself

If you can afford to have it done professionally, do so. Packing is not expensive. BAR companies use a range of appropriate packing materials and employ fully trained staff that will pack your things professionally and safely. Only goods that are packed professionally can be covered fully by insurance.

Take out insurance

No matter how much care is taken with packing and handling, accidents do sometimes happen. All BAR members are able to offer insurance and we strongly advise you to discuss this with them.

Don't move on Friday

If you can, avoid Fridays as this day is always busy. Some moving companies may even offer a discount if you move in the middle of the week.

BAR members can be accessed via the website **www.bar.co.uk**, or If you need advice, contact BAR on **0208 861 3331**. (See advertisement opposite for more information).

Moving home? If you're choosing a removals company...

choose a professional.

Moving home is stressful enough without worrying about who's doing what and when on the big day. There's the safety of your personal and cherished belongings to consider as they're being packed, loaded, transported and delivered. And then there's storage!

So who should you go to when choosing the right removals company?

The British Association of Removers (BAR) is the largest established and recognised Trade Association for removals companies.

All member companies must meet strict standards and agree to inspection on a regular basis to ensure that their facilities, equipment and expertise remain at the highest level. In fact, fewer than 700 removals companies in the whole of the UK can claim to be members.

Many of our members are also accredited with the European Quality Standard for Removals: BS EN 12522.

● All member companies must use trained staff and appropriate vehicles.

● They must provide written quotations before any work is undertaken and offer service schedules and plain English contracts to ensure any confusion is avoided.

● All member companies must offer suitable insurance and are able to offer a 3 month emergency service guarantee. Just ask for Careline.

If you're planning on using a removals company, be sure to approach one you can trust.

Look for the badge.

British Association of Removers
3 Churchill Court
58 Station Road
North Harrow
HA2 7SA

T 020 8861 3331
F 020 8861 3332
E info@bar.co.uk

For more information go to **www.bar.co.uk**

Find a house and make a bid

Offer what you think the property is worth. Make the offer subject to a survey of the property. If the price is marginally above a stamp duty cut-off point (see table below), offer slightly below this amount to save money. Where necessary, exclude the cost of carpets, curtains and other fixtures from the purchase price to do this.

Stamp duty	£ (%)
Up to £60,000	nil
£60,001 to £250,000	1%
£250,001 to £500,000	3%
£500,001 and above	4%

Contact lender and arrange survey

Once you have had an offer accepted, you need to finalise details with your lender and organise a survey. There are three main types of survey:

■ The lender will demand a Mortgage Valuation. You will normally pay for this, but it is commissioned by the lender. It's a brief report on the property you plan to buy, basically telling the lender whether or not it is worth the money you have offered.

■ It's highly advisable to commission your own survey, known as a Homebuyer's Report. This is likely to cost two or three hundred pounds, but it's much more detailed than the valuation and it's a direct contract between you and the surveyor. This should pick up any problems – like a bad roof or damp – that might lead you to lower the offer you've made on the property. You can ask the lender's surveyor to make a Homebuyer's Report at the same time he or she does the valuation. Or you can commission an independent surveyor.

▌ For complete peace of mind a full Structural Survey may be necessary. This is the most expensive kind of survey, but it includes full details of all visible parts of the house, and highlights defects.

All surveyors only look at visible things – they don't lift carpets, for example – so you may well move into your new home and find things that have not been picked up.

Some surveyors in 'hot spots' such as London will value property at less than its market price. This is a problem for you if you are borrowing a high percentage of the cost of the property, because the lender will go on the surveyor's valuation – not what you have paid in the real market. You may end up losing the property, or being asked to pay a high lending fee (also known as a mortgage indemnity guarantee).

Think about what you need from a surveyor

Before you fork out, it is worth taking the time to think about what it is you want the survey to tell you.

Your requirements will be different if you are simply moving house than if you are looking to renovate or restore a property.

If you do have a specific requirement from your surveyor, for example, if you are buying an older home or a listed building, it is worthwhile finding a surveyor who has some degree of experience or speciality in that field.

What can a surveyor do?

If you have any plans for renovating the property, your surveyor is the best source of information for the viability of the work you plan. He or she can provide you with information and advice about:

▌ planning permission – What are the restrictions? Are there any fees?

Choosing a trustworthy removal company

There is no UK legislation governing the removals industry, so you run the risk of entrusting your precious possessions to an incompetent amateur or, worse still, a rogue. To find a safe and professional remover, you should contact The National Guild of Removers and Storers.

Established in 1991, the Guild is recognised by *Which?* Magazine as being at the forefront of consumer protection in the industry. Move with a Guild member and you will benefit from four **unique and exclusive** consumer protection programmes:

- Members of The Guild are also members of The Removals Industry Ombudsman Scheme, the ultimate consumer protection in the removals industry.

- Members of The Guild are subject to an independent annual inspection by The National Register of Approved Removers and Storers. For your peace of mind a copy of the inspector's report is supplied with your quotation.

- Members of The Guild are licensed to offer The Removal Protection Bond – a 'no fault' insurance product that covers you against a number of unforeseen problems that may occur on moving day. For example, should completion not take place, the Bond pays up to £1500 towards extra removal, storage and other specified incidental costs.

- Members of The Guild are continually monitored by quality questionnaires, issued to every customer.

Don't be fooled by low prices. Choose a remover who can prove they are reliable and professional. Your home is worth it!

For details of your local Guild members, call **01494 792279**.

For a safe move,

choose a member of The National Guild of Removers and Storers.

OMBUDSMAN SCHEME MEMBER

- demolition and erection of structural walls and other major changes;
- listed building regulations – guidelines and limitations;
- conservation area regulations and levels of restriction;
- safety issues.

Finding a surveyor

If you have chosen to undertake a survey of a property independently of your mortgage provider, it is worth spending the time making sure the surveyor will provide what you need from a survey.

Surveys are expensive and can be very important when deciding whether to go ahead with a sale so don't be afraid to ask questions. Many surveyors have areas of speciality, which may suit your needs better. For example, they may specialise in listed buildings or auction properties.

Chartered Surveyors

Members and Affiliates of the Royal Institution of Chartered Surveyors (RICS) can be identified by the letters MRICS and FRICS (Fellow of the Royal Institution of Chartered Surveyors) after their name. They are the only people allowed to call themselves Chartered Surveyors or Chartered Building Surveyors.

Home Information Packs

Government proposals for Home Information Packs could change the way we buy and sell property in England and Wales. The aim is to shift responsibility for gathering information and getting a survey done from the buyer to the seller, and thereby speed up the buying process. But, of course, this will cost, and the current price quoted is between £700 and £1,200 to sell the average home. Most estate agents are against the idea, describing it as bureaucratic and unenforceable. They say the expense of a HIP will put people off moving. The government has already been forced to back down on one key proposal – ministers have cancelled plans to make it a criminal offence to advertise a house for sale without a current SP. The target introduction date has not yet been finalised, but is likely to be sometime during 2006.

Exchange contracts/complete

The standard gap between exchanging contracts and completion is 30 days, but it can be longer or shorter. You can ask your solicitor to put a clause into the contract stipulating a time limit. Points to check include the following:

■ Make sure that all the legal paperwork is properly sorted. Don't be afraid to ask about any point you don't understand. If you have paid a deposit (usually between 5 and 10 per cent) you will lose it if you pull out after exchange.

■ Check and check again that the funds are ready to be paid by your lender into the vendor's account, via your solicitor. Failure to do so means you won't be able to move in.

You are now ready to move into your house. You should already have hired a removal firm. Be sure to compare prices and make sure your chosen firm is insured if anything is lost or broken.

Contact electricity, gas, water and phone companies to let them know you are moving to a new address – give meter readings for both the old and the new address. Now is the time to decide who you want to supply your energy, water and phone needs at your new address.

Completion will take place when all legal questions have been agreed and the cash has been passed on to the seller from your lender, via your own and his/her solicitor.

8 Buy-to-let

Buying property to let is becoming increasingly popular. There's now a whole army of amateur landlords out there depending on their investment in bricks and mortar to finance their retirement.

Low mortgage rates and the availability of buy-to-let mortgages have made it an option for many more people. The main attraction is the potential for a better return than on other investments like stocks and shares.

What you might get back

You can expect rental income to provide a return on your investment of 7 or 8 per cent on average, before costs.

You may also make a capital gain on your property. Property prices generally rise faster than inflation, and have averaged a gain of 8.9 per cent a year over the last 25 years. However, this also includes a period in the late-1980s/early-1990s when prices fell.

Using a mortgage to fund your purchase gives you a 'geared' investment that can magnify returns enormously. For example, say you put down a deposit of £10,000 on a £100,000 property, the rent covers all outgoings, and after five years you sell the property for £150,000. The gains you have made before tax are £50,000. This equals a return of 500 per cent on your original investment.

There is a risk, though. Gearing magnifies losses as well. If property prices fall, you could go into negative equity, owing more on your mortgage than the property is worth.

Do your sums

The possibility of falling property prices is only one of the factors you need to consider. There are plenty of others that will have an impact on any total return to be made on property. Here are some of them:

▌ *Agency fees*: using a letting agent to manage your property will cost between 10 and 15 per cent of rental income.

▌ *Income tax*: rent counts as income, which you should declare on a self-assessment tax form each year. You can offset various expenses against tax, including mortgage interest, agent's fees, the cost of repairs, and expenses associated with a leasehold flat (typically ground rent, service charges and buildings insurance).

▌ *Capital gains tax (CGT)*: if the property is not your main place of residence you may be liable to CGT on any profit you make when it is sold. There are some exemptions that could apply to you. Talk to a tax specialist.

▌ *Insurance*: lenders will almost certainly require extra cover if you propose to let the property. It is generally at least 50 per cent dearer than normal home and contents insurance.

▌ *Maintenance*: most property letting agents advise that at least 10 per cent of monthly income ought to be kept back for property repairs and maintenance.

▌ *Void periods*: this is the time between tenancies when you will not be able to collect any rent. Agents suggest you allow for a void period of two months in each year.

▌ *A rise in interest rates*: will you be able to meet the extra costs if this happens – or raise your tenants' rent to cover your costs?

▌ *Diversification*: consider if you want such a sizeable chunk of your total wealth portfolio to be in property.

Thinking of letting your property?

If so, for peace of mind use an agent who is a member of
The National Approved Letting Scheme.

The National Approved Letting Scheme (NALS) is a voluntary
accreditation scheme for lettings and management agents. It was
established in 1999 with the objective of giving owners the
confidence to let their property by appointing qualified agents who
in joining the Scheme, have agreed to abide by a set of minimum
service standards for letting and management.

The NALS Scheme was set up to provide much needed benchmark
service standards that would enable landlords and tenants to avoid
the pitfalls of dealing with rogue letting agents.

The Scheme backed by the Government and the professional bodies
in the lettings sector ARLA (Association of Residential Letting
Agents), NAEA (National Association of Estate Agents) and RICS
(Royal Institution of Chartered Surveyors) is open to any agent in the
lettings sector who meets the strict criteria for accreditation.

It is a prerequisite of membership that firms should have in place a
customer complaints procedure underpinned by an arbitration
scheme, Professional Indemnity insurance and Client Money
Protection insurance which ensures that clients' money is protected.

*For further information on NALS and to obtain details of an agent in
your area contact:*
The National Approved Letting Scheme
Tavistock House
5 Rodney Road
Cheltenham GL50 1HX
T: 01242 581712 F: 01242 232518
E-mail: info@nalscheme.co.uk
Website: www.nalscheme.co.uk

You must take a long-term view if you decide to buy a property to rent out. A minimum of five years is a good rule of thumb – it is not a way of getting rich quick. The above questions don't negate the value of property as an investment, so don't let the issues put you off, but do think carefully before making such an important decision.

Common mistakes

There are three mistakes amateur landlords are most likely to make:

First mistake

The first mistake most of them make is looking and buying a property they would like to live in themselves. But the rental market is different from the owner-occupied market and tenants don't want the same things as owners. Buying a property to rent out as an investment is a business decision. Buying a home to live in is an emotional decision. The two are not the same.

For example, tenants don't look for 'character', 'original fixtures', 'history' or 'community feeling'. They do care about good public transport links, size of bedrooms (important when it comes to splitting the rent) and being able to move straight in to a low maintenance place.

Second mistake

Most amateur landlords spend too much money fitting out their property. Especially if the house or flat is to be rented out to two or more tenants, most items will have to be replaced after each tenancy ends and the place redecorated. This is not because the tenants will be irresponsible or wreckers, but simply because of wear and tear. And you are much more likely to rent it quickly if would-be tenants are impressed by a freshly-decorated, spick and span place.

Dos and don'ts include:

I   Don't spend money on an expensive dinner service – just go to a High Street shop and buy plain white china.

I   Don't spend time agonising over paint colours – just decorate with white paint throughout.

I   Don't buy top-of-the-range beds and mattresses expecting them to last – buy a cheap mattress at the beginning of each tenancy.

I   Do spend money on a decent shower. If the bathroom needs replacing do it with a white suite.

I   Don't bother with carpet. Tiles or easily-replaceable and cleaned lino is better.

I   Do update the kitchen if it needs it – again keep it simple.

I   Do comply with all safety regulations and make sure every-thing works – the heating, the electrics, the oven – and do get all the relevant safety checks done by a CORGI registered gas engineer. All the furniture also has to comply with the Furnishings Fire and Safety Regulations 1988. Make sure everything you buy – mattresses, sofas, curtains and uphol-stery – have passed the flammability tests and are labelled as such. The fine for not doing so is £5,000. Don't forget smoke detectors and fire extinguishers either.

Third mistake

Many new landlords think they can find the tenants themselves. They either want to save the money a letting agency would charge or they have a friend of a friend move in. But using an approved letting agent is the best way of ensuring that any prospective tenant is financially sound, with all references properly checked. This sets you up for a hassle-free tenancy.

There are two organisations – the Association of Residential Lettings Agents (ARLA) and the National Approved Lettings Scheme (NALS) – that offer protection to landlords and tenants from cowboy rental companies. The average fee is 10 per cent to find and check out a tenant, get the deposit and draw up the tenancy agreement. That's a small price to pay for peace of mind.

Remember, renting out a property is a formal business arrangement. Even the friend of a friend should sign a standard rental agreement. An Assured Shorthold Tenancy contract means that you can give the tenant notice to quit after six months if something goes wrong. You can buy them from good stationers.

At the end of the tenancy be fair and realistic about returning the renter's deposit. The deposit is usually between six and eight weeks' rent so it's a sizeable sum. You cannot hold back £50 because the number of spoons is down. You can withhold the cost of having the place cleaned if it's left dirty on departure. You cannot charge the tenant for normal wear and tear – be professional.

Watch out for new rules and regulations

Regulations going through parliament may make it more expensive for small landlords to let their properties. Some industry experts say the regulations – contained in a private member's bill with Government support – could lead to the closure of some of Britain's estimated 1.5 million 'houses in multiple occupation', or HMOs. These are defined as properties occupied 'by persons who do not form a single household'. There are eight types but they fit into two broad categories:

- houses converted into bed-sits, flats or private rooms with communal areas but just one front door and one landlord;

- unconverted houses with individuals having their own rooms, but almost all other spaces shared by three or more people, such as students or young professionals.

The Department of Transport, Local Government and the Regions (DTLR), which oversees regulation for the private rented sector, saw most of these measures mentioned in the Queen's Speech last year (2003) and they are likely to become law if there is enough Parliamentary time.

Landlords or managing agents will have to fit extensive health and safety measures, which may include additional bathrooms, fire escapes and energy conservation features. It also introduces a national licensing system for HMOs, making safety checks and a licence mandatory before a landlord can rent to sharers.

Property professionals say the measures will be useful for forcing up the standards of unscrupulous landlords who exploit vulnerable tenants, but some fear they may deter small investors who buy-to-let as an alternative to a pension, as well as those who take lodgers. More licence fees, more regulations and more work required will eat into profit margins unless rents are raised.

Taxes

The downside of investing in property is that all forms of income, including that from bricks and mortar, are liable for income tax. And if the rental property is sold, any profit may also be subject to capital gains tax. But the upside is that landlords can deduct a number of expenses from the rent that tenants pay, so only the profit is taxed.

The tax return deadline

If you receive any income at all from property, you must remember to fill out the relevant land and property pages on your tax return and submit it all to the Inland Revenue by 31 January. This is the date when any tax you owe must also be paid; otherwise you'll face a fine and possible surcharges.

Everyone who had an income from property in the year running from 6 April 2001 to 5 April 2002 should have received a tax return. This comprises the standard form plus additional property pages. If you haven't received all this, get in touch with the Revenue immediately, as not receiving a tax return is not a legitimate excuse for failing to submit it on time.

Getting started

Once you have the forms you need, filling them out should be straightforward as long as you have all your accounts, bank statements and receipts to hand. If your gross income from property was less than £15,000, it should be even easier as all you have to supply is a figure for your total profit (income less expenses).

All rental activities are aggregated and treated as if they constitute a single business, so if you have several properties, the income and costs from all of them should be added together. The advantage of this arrangement is that if you made a big profit on one address, it should go some way to balancing out the losses made on another.

All rent, whether from furnished or unfurnished property, is regarded as income, as are separate charges to tenants for the hiring of furniture, and service charges to meet the landlord's responsibility for maintaining common parts of a building.

Deductible expenses

It is possible to reduce your taxable profit via a number of deductible expenses. The rent is included in this but the cost of buying the property isn't. Most landlords opt for an interest-only mortgage because all your monthly payments can be offset against tax.

With a repayment mortgage, where part of the capital is paid back along with interest on the loan each month, it is still possible to deduct expenses but only from the interest part – and the sums become more complicated. Several expenses are normally deductible when calculating the profits of your rental business. Council tax, insurance premiums – both buildings and contents insurance and cover for the non-payment of rent – and advertising costs can all be claimed.

Travelling expenses incurred by the landlord when checking the property, to carry out repairs or collect the rent, are also allowable deductions. If you travel by car, it is likely that you are also using it at other times, in which case you have to work out the proportion of the running costs attributable to business use.

Repairs or improvements?

The cost of repairs can be claimed back against the rent, but landlords need to be careful because capital expenditure, in the form of most improvements, isn't tax deductible. For example, if you touch up the property with a lick of paint when you first buy it, you can claim the cost of this back against the rent. But if you buy a dilapidated property that requires thousands of pounds' worth of work before you can let it, the cost of those improvements is regarded as a capital expense and can't be claimed against the rent.

In general, any work that isn't strictly necessary but increases the value of the property, such as a new fitted kitchen or conservatory, is considered to be capital expenditure and can't be claimed back.

Furnished property

If your property is furnished, there are other allowable expenses. You can't claim for the cost of actually buying the beds, sofa or washing machine, but you can claim the subsequent cost of replacing damaged or worn-out furniture and furnishings.

Landlords can choose to deduct 10 per cent of the rent, net of council tax, from income as a wear-and-tear allowance. Or you can deduct the full cost of renewing individual items such as chairs and rugs, as and when the expenditure is incurred. Whichever method you choose, it must be used consistently and you are not allowed to chop and change from year to year.

Making life easier

One way to minimise the hassle of keeping your own accounts is to employ a letting agent. This can be time and cost effective because as they are managing the property for you, they will also be able to tell you how much income you have received and what expenses have been incurred.

Many people are put off employing a letting agent by the costs involved, which can be up to 15 per cent of the rent for a full management service. However, these fees are tax deductible, so you can both get your money back and reduce the accounting hassle.

Going it alone shouldn't be a problem as long as you protect yourself by maintaining accurate records and keeping all receipts, bank statements and invoices for at least six years – the Revenue can make random enquiries of any taxpayer.

What happens when you sell?

Your 'principal private residence' is exempt from capital gains tax (CGT), but higher-rate taxpayers are potentially liable for CGT at 40 per cent on the profits from the sale of a holiday cottage or a buy-to-let property. Basic-rate taxpayers pay CGT at 20 per cent.

However, there is an easy way to cut – or even eliminate – your tax bill. If you have two properties, you can choose which is your main residence for tax purposes. But you must make your choice within two years of buying the second home – and you must at some point have lived in the property.

As long as you meet the deadline, you can change your mind later and elect the other property – with no time limit. The rule means that you may be able to minimise CGT on the sale of a second home.

Tax pitfalls

According to the Council of Mortgage Lenders, over a million households in England – 5.6 per cent of the total – already own second homes. However, this doesn't take into account professional property investors, and the recent growth in buy-to-let. The Association of Residential Landlords estimate a further 250,000 residential buy-to-let owners and an unknown number of landlords who own their property outright.

This surge has created a capital gains tax and inheritance problem for owners. The biggest problem is inheritance tax, given that the average property is now valued at £128,000. If you own two properties, you are almost certainly over the threshold for IHT – £255,000 for the current tax year (2003–04).

You can avoid liability by giving away your assets and, provided you survive for another seven years, the assets are outside your estate for IHT purposes. However, there are problems giving away property.

A gift of property is considered a disposal for CGT purposes, and tax is payable at the time you make the gift. Married couples can transfer assets between themselves without incurring a CGT liability, but when the property is sold, or given to the children, CGT is calculated from the date of acquisition by the first partner.

It also doesn't help much for the parent to sell and give their child money. If a widow gives her holiday home to her son, she will pay CGT on any profit made from the date of acquisition to the date of making the gift. She will be entitled to indexation relief up to April 1998 and taper relief thereafter, but she still has to pay the tax on making the gift. If this property is then held by the son as a holiday home or investment, he will pay CGT on any increase in value from the time of the gift until the property is sold.

You might decide, when buying a second home, to put it in your and your children's names. But does this get caught by the 'gifts with reservation' rules if you use it as a holiday home? Apparently not – at least for the moment. Where joint ownership is involved, each joint owner has a legal right to live in the house, so there is no reservation of benefit. If the children are minors, trust arrangements will be necessary, as minors are not permitted to own interests in land. All joint owners must use the property and if one ceases to use the house, a gift with reservation situation could arise at that point.

If a part share of a house is transferred to children this way, and there's no gift with reservation, then it will be a potentially exempt transfer for IHT and there'll be no IHT on the transfer, if the donor survives for at least seven years. Only the value of the part retained would form part of the donor's estate on death.

The interaction of IHT and CGT must be considered. Making such a gift reduces the IHT on death, at the expense of CGT. Also, assuming house prices keep rising, the children will have a lower base cost for CGT purposes, as they will have had part of the property earlier, and at a lower value than they would on death.

Although IHT and CGT are nominally charged at 40 per cent, taper relief is available on capital gains, potentially reducing the effective rate to 24 per cent for assets owned for 10 years or more.

For sellers of a second property during their lifetime, there are ways of mitigating CGT on a property. Until April 1998, index-ation allowance meant that only profit over and above inflation, and after any relevant capital expenditure, was subject to CGT. So if you bought a property in 1990 for £100,000 and sold it in March 1998 for £200,000, the acquisition price of the property would be index-linked to the retail prices index. This would give you a 'real' acquisition cost of about £150,000 because inflation over the period was about 50 per cent. You would then pay CGT on the real profit of £50,000. And you would be able to offset your annual CGT allowance against the £50,000 profit. A married couple who owned a second home jointly would both be able to use their annual CGT allowance to reduce the tax still further.

For non-business assets, which would normally include a buy-to-let property, the proportion of any gain subject to CGT falls from 100 per cent to 60 per cent over 10 years. For higher-rate taxpayers this means you effectively pay CGT at 24 per cent after 10 years. With canny planning it may be possible to avoid CGT altogether.

And where a gain is made on disposal of a property that has been a main residence at some point, but has also been let specifically as residential accommodation, there is a further special relief on gains of up to 40,000.

Unmarried couples can nominate a home as their main residence – even if it is only used at weekends. Married couples who jointly own a property can claim two potential sets of annual CGT allowance and switch the main residence to the most appropriate property.

You can avoid CGT completely if you retire abroad for at least five years. If you leave the UK having been resident for any part of at least four of the previous seven tax years, then return within five tax years (known as being 'temporarily non-resident'), you could be liable to CGT on the sale of UK assets. Until the five years limit is up you will still be liable to CGT on gains made while abroad, on assets held before you left the UK, even if you sold them after you left. Gains will be taxed in the tax year you resume UK residence. To be certain of avoiding CGT, you must first become non-resident, then sell the properties, and not return to the UK within five years. Remember though, that you could be liable to CGT on the sale of UK assets in your new country of residence – and at a higher rate than in the UK.

For more information contact: the Association of Residential Letting Agents (ARLA), www.arla.co.uk or 0845 345 5752; www.inlandrevenue.gov.uk or try its self-assessment helpline on 0845 900 0444, open evenings and weekends.

9 Self-build

Building your own home

Self-build is a tiny part of the housing market in the UK. Last year, the Nationwide, Britain's biggest building society, financed just 600 projects throughout the country. But the idea of building your own home is becoming increasingly popular as we strive to find the house of our dreams. Between 20,000 and 25,000 people build their own homes every year, and of those 90 per cent have never built anything before.

How to get a self-build mortgage

Most of us delude ourselves into believing we own our house. Of course, that's not true. The lender owns it usually for the first 25 years we live there. A bank or a building society pays upfront and then sells the place back to you in stages, so that you can move in decades before you'd otherwise have been able to afford to.

But if, as is the case with a self-build, there's no house for the mortgage lender to buy upfront, you can forgive them for wondering where their money's going. You're going to have to do a lot more talking than usual to convince them you're a good risk.

Lenders, perhaps justifiably, believe more can go wrong with a self-build than a traditional house purchase. This is why self-build mortgages come with a much tighter web of checks and controls. Many lenders won't give you a penny until your building is up to first-floor level.

Grand designs

Whatever you're planning, we'll help you find the right mortgage.

Call into any
Lloyds TSB Scotland
branch for details of our
Self-build mortgages.

MORTGAGES WORTH TALKING ABOUT

 Lloyds TSB Scotland

How Do Self-Build Mortgages Work?

– by Norrie Henderson, Head of Mortgages for LloydsTSB Scotland

The popularity of terrestrial and satellite TV shows about DIY and dissatisfaction with the limited range of most new-build houses are proving to be key driving forces behind the fast growing phenomenon that is seeing thousands of people taking up the challenge of building the home of their dreams.

There are many types of people who embark on the self-build route – from young families wanting a larger house than they could normally afford and people wanting to build their dream home for retirement, to people that self-build for profit and those who want to live an environmentally-friendly lifestyle.

Whatever the reason, it is absolutely essential that people considering self-build get the planning, both logistical and financial, absolutely right.

One of Scotland's leading mortgage experts and someone who has gone down the self-build route himself, is Norrie Henderson, Head of Mortgages for LloydsTSB Scotland – an acknowledged specialist in the field of Self-Build Mortgage products. In this feature, Norrie Henderson shares his experiences and knowledge – pointing out the key facets of a self-build project and how a Self-Build Mortgage works.

"First, I would like to point out that whilst the product is called a Self-Build Mortgage, it doesn't mean that people have to carry out all the building work themselves! In fact, if someone proposed to carry out all the work on their own, it would set a few alarm bells ringing!

*"There are several things a lender looks for when interviewing self-build customers and, without doubt, a major attribute I look for is **commitment**.*

"People need to show detailed research and planning, that the property would realise the value of the mortgage and that the building costs are accurate.

"Once the mortgage is agreed, planning permission is sought. During this process – which can take up to thirteen weeks – identify your potential suppliers and request quotes. Ask for two or three quotes – there may be a significant variation due to location and availability."

Benchmarks
Money is released in stages:
1. Purchase of the plot
2. Foundations being laid
3. Wind and water stage – shell complete and interior protected from the elements
4. Completion – the most expensive stage, where plumbing, power, decoration, fittings etc are all installed.

Money is released in a timely manner subject to a revaluation as each stage is completed. However, in some cases, people take out indemnity insurance which enables them to release the cash before each stage – this can help them realise cost savings from paying cash-in-hand, taking advantage of sales, auctions etc.

If people wish to vary the plans during the build process, for example, to change from four to three larger bedrooms, lenders will agree as long as the proposed variation doesn't impact too negatively on the potential value of the property. Also, Building Control will have to pass the changes.

Diligence

When appointing subcontractors it is absolutely vital to understand exactly what work is included within the costs quoted. Make sure that all work quoted is detailed in a written and signed proposal. A real example of how this can work against you is where a builder charges extra for putting in a front doorstep and path saying that they weren't included in the original quote. On another build, the owner found out that none of the electrical materials were included – just the labour cost. Therefore, never make assumptions about the detail of a quote – understand exactly what you are getting.

Another area where people make assumptions is on the costs of items such as fitted kitchens or bathroom suites. Builders will often allow a standard amount for these items in their quote – but if you choose a luxury bathroom suite and a top-of-the-range fitted kitchen – you could find yourself a few thousand pounds over budget. Always discuss with the builder what cost contingency is in the plan for these items and then you can make a decision based on knowledge not assumptions.

It is imperative that all the trades-people you engage are members of reputable trade bodies and all materials you use must comply to recognised building standards. Never cut corners – Building Control will never allow substandard materials to be used.

Help

Specialist companies are available to help people through the self-build process and often act as links between customer and lender. They provide checklists, preferred suppliers lists and help you find the right lender for your self-build mortgage.

Summary

Almost all self-build projects are successful and completed within the projected timescale.

Self-builders get a great sense of achievement after completion – and why not, they have just built their dream home and, in most cases, are now the proud owners of a property that is worth 25% to 40% more than the cost of building it!

Lenders generally won't give you a cheque for the cost of buying some land and building a house, and then leave you to get on with it. Often they will expect you to have found and bought the land already.

Some lenders refuse to handover any cash for the site. If they are willing to do so, it's unlikely to be more than 75 per cent, but at least that way you know they're interested in doing business with self-builders.

Your ultimate aim is to get the best deal on offer so you have to look for a variety of features, not least the amount they're willing to lend you in the first place. Each lender has a percentage of your property's projected value it is willing to stump up – this is known as the loan to value ratio (LTV), and will typically be around 75 to 95 per cent.

As with all other mortgages, the lender will only give you a loan it's confident you'll be able to repay, so look at three times your own annual income, plus one times your partner's, if applicable, and that's your maximum loan.

A good way of finding out about all the deals on offer is to get hold of a monthly magazine called *Moneyfacts*. It's available by subscription from your local newsagents. *Moneyfacts* will tell you exactly what rates are on offer from the various lenders, allowing you to weigh up the alternatives.

As a self-builder you need to ask a lot more questions because mortgage companies like to tailor each deal to the individual project. This is their way of making sure their investment is sound. The most obvious way they can do this is by strong control of the purse strings. Self-build mortgages pay out in stages. Each lender does this a different way, but typical stages include the completion of foundations, weatherproofing, damp course, first floor and so on. These are usually called 'progress' or 'instalment' mortgages.

The theory is that this way, you're given just enough money to stay ahead of the game, while the lender's commitment only goes up as the value of your site increases. The majority of failures among self-build mortgages happen at this stage – and it's not normally the self-builder's fault. Contractors going bust is the main problem.

Once the house is complete, you can move over to a traditional repayment plan, taking up the mortgage to suit your needs.

One of the most self-build-friendly lenders is the Bradford & Bingley, which recognises the unique problems associated with building your own home. 'Cash flow has dogged self-builders for years,' says the company's specialist in the field. 'It's been a question of beg, borrow and steal money to see you through until you can get the funds released.'

In response, it set up what it calls an Accelerator Mortgage, in conjunction with the Self-Build Advisory Service (SBAS). This enables self-builders to borrow up to 95 per cent of the build costs. Normally, if, for example, you're buying a kit home, you have to finance the purchase of the kit before it's been erected. With this mortgage, once the kit has been delivered on site, they'll advance 95 per cent of the cost of purchasing it. This gets over a lot of cash-flow problems.

Other costs

Apart from the price of the plot and your build costs, other expenses to take into consideration are architect's fees, service connections, special groundworks, garden landscaping, insurance and administration costs.

The fee for drawing up your house plans can vary from a few hundred pounds, if done by a draftsman, to several thousand if you decide to use an architect.

Expect to pay at least £1000 for connection fees to electricity, water, sewerage and gas, and considerably more if your plot is off the beaten track.

Steep sites and soft ground can create problems requiring specialist foundations so this should be taken into account as well.

Landscaping for your garden is usually best done at the outset so should also be included in the equation.

Another hefty expense is the cost of insurance, which will probably set you back around £1,500.

Finally, remember that while all the building is going on you will need to live somewhere – rented accommodation or an on-site caravan. These costs also should be taken into account and there are several excellent software packages to help you calculate your costs and projected cash-flow.

Finding a plot

Finding a plot for your new house can be a frustrating and time-consuming process. Also, it is very much a case of chicken and egg. Which comes first – finding a plot and then choosing a house design or choosing the house design and finding a plot that suits it?

Both methods have their 'pros' and 'cons'. What use is a plot in an excellent location if it isn't wide enough for your new home? Or you could plan your dream mansion and never find a plot that will do it justice.

As always the answer is to compromise. Look for plots and consider the type of house that can be built on it. In many cases a plot may be found between two other houses, in which case planning permission may only be granted if your home fits in with local architecture. What benefit is there in having a plan for a contemporary glass and steel structure when it will sit between two thatched cottages?

The size of the plot required can be predicted by knowing how big the house will be and whether you need a large garden or a garage.

So, what should you consider as the most important aspect of your plot? The answer to this will also influence how you find your plot – location. If you want to live locally, you have an advantage in that you will probably know who the local estate agents are, receive the local paper and may even see plots for sale as you drive around. If your chosen area is on the other side of the country, you will need to investigate the available plot-finding resources very carefully.

Where to find a plot

The obvious first place to look for plots is the estate agents. The large chains may be helpful if your plot searching campaign is centred elsewhere in the country, as they can put you in touch with their other offices.

Some estate agents have extensive lists of plots and go to a great deal of trouble to provide information, pictures and maps of where they are. Others either have no plots at all or regard them as a secondary issue to selling houses. The larger chains will often have a 'land and new homes division', while the smaller agents may not sell a plot from one year to the next.

Don't be content being put on an agent's mailing list. Keep in regular contact with them, especially just prior to the local newspaper going on sale – any new plots they are to advertise in the paper can be checked out before the rest of the readership even knows about it.

Surveyors, architects, architectural technicians and planning consultants can also provide leads on land for sale. Such professions revolve around building sites and future developments. Chances are one of them might know of something in the pipeline.

It's the same for friends, neighbours and colleagues. If you tell enough people that you are looking for a plot in a particular area, someone somewhere will know about one, or suggest a potential site. A conversation in the pub over a pint could end months of searching. It's worth a try.

The local newspapers advertise plots of land but you have to be quick to get the good ones. You could always run a 'building plot wanted' advertisement in the paper. State what you want, for example, a plot suitable for a bungalow, with planning permission, rural location, and where you want it. Not only will those people with plots for sale be interested, but those with land not yet for sale may contact you out of the blue.

Check also the official notices in the classified section. Many councils put notices of planning applications in the local papers in addition to posting notices of the application to the neighbours of the site. As a result, you may be able to scoop a plot before it goes on the market.

Auctions

Newspapers will also advertise forthcoming auctions in your area. Often sourced from bankruptcies and mortgage foreclosures, this is a chance to find plots that would not ordinarily come on to the market and may be cheaper than market value.

To find out about what is coming up for sale in the next few weeks, Faxwise (020 7720 5000) provides a subscription service called 'auction watch', which will inform you of any lots. *SelfBuild & Design* contains a comprehensive list of plot details in the back of each issue. It is an invaluable guide to land prices and availability in all areas of the country, as well as a listing of those estate agents who deal with building land.

If your house is to be built by a package company, it is in their interests for you to find a plot. Some companies have land lists. Speak to them to see if they can offer assistance in finding a plot, but don't let their answer cloud your judgement. Just because they know of plots for sale doesn't mean they can build the right house for you.

Exhibitors at the various self-build shows and exhibitions may also have local knowledge of plots. The more local the show, the greater the chance of coming across a contact.

Builders and developers are self-builders on a major scale. They buy in bulk, purchasing development sites of several acres to build a set number of homes. In many cases they will have a few spaces on the site that are not utilised in their plans. These present ideal opportunities for the canny self-builder, as the developer will receive cash for a piece of land they were going to leave bare, while you get a plot, often with planning permission and services on site.

Councils also own areas of land that they sell off occasionally for extra cash. In some cases, tenancy of the land has ended and the council will prefer to sell. In other cases, council policy may change, prompting the sale. The council may also own buildings that can be converted or renovated. Call the estates department to find out if any property is coming up for sale in the near future.

Utility companies and large businesses may also have land for sale. Railtrack, British Gas, the electricity and water companies, even breweries often have land surplus to requirements.

Finally, if your own efforts fail, try the professionals. There are several plotfinding companies that will produce a list of plots to meet your criteria – for a fee. At the end of the day, there is no secret to finding your ideal plot. Some self-builders find land amazingly easily and can start their project straight away. Others may look for several years. Whatever the circumstances, perseverance is vital.

Planning permission

Plots with planning permission are more expensive as they have already been permitted to become potential homes. A plot without planning permission is just a bare piece of land. Don't be fooled into buying it on the off-chance you can build on it. If it's not sold with outline planning permission, the vendor is missing out on extra cash so there must be a reason for it.

What is it?

There are two types of planning permission – outline (OPP) and detailed (DPP). Outline, as its name implies, means that the planning department has agreed the basics of a development proposal. The usual routine is that once OPP has been granted, you apply for DPP or reserved matters. This is only given when the planning department has agreed exactly what can be built on your plot using your detailed house plans as their guide. Even building materials and height can influence a decision at this point.

So if you are trying to get DPP why bother going through the process of applying for OPP? In many cases plots will already have OPP, which means that while the plot can be built on, the style of house remains open. Alternatively, applying for OPP will save you the cost of having expensive house plans drawn up before you are even sure you are allowed to build at all.

With OPP you can put forward as many detailed applications as you like. An interesting point is that you don't have to own the land to make an application, so you can find out if you can build on a plot before making an offer on it.

Once you have OPP, you have three years in which to make reserved matters before having to re-apply. Reserved matters is the term for a follow-on application to outline planning. Detailed planning, however, can slightly alter what was originally proposed as the planning committee will reassess the application. Having gained DPP you have five years in which to begin work on a development.

Even with OPP, detailed planning doesn't always come easy. Permission usually depends on a number of conditions, such as the colour of brick, the type of roofing material, even the size and location of windows. These conditions usually come about due to the council's concern that new housing will look out of place or interfere with established homes.

How do you get it?

Firstly, you need to apply for it. In theory, this is just a case of filling in some forms, but the reality is that this matter deserves plenty of time and effort to get it right first time. Having decided what you want, a house of a particular size or an extension for example, you can do plenty of research prior doing the actual paperwork.

The Local Plan at your council's planning office will show you what areas are deigned as favourable for development. Make sure your proposals fall into line with it, and while there is a chance that the plan will change, these things tend to take a very long time.

Professionals such as building surveyors, architects or architectural technicians will be helpful at this early stage to guide you through the intricacies of the planning process and later prepare technical drawings.

You should also contact the local planning officer to discuss the proposal prior to application. This will give you an insight into how favourably the planning department will look on your application. If you are using an architect or surveyor, bring them along to the meeting. You should receive some feedback with suggestions as to what might need re-thinking – blocking light into a neighbour's living room, for example.

Detailed planning permission has a standard fee for each dwelling, whereas outline planning is charged depending upon the size of the proposed development site.

With the application you should state whether you own all, part or none of the site and whether it has agricultural tenancy. If you are not the sole owner, then the actual owner must be notified of your intention.

A location map, usually OS 1:2,500 or 1:1,250, should accompany the application. For DPP, a site plan should also be included, alongside floor plans and all elevations showing the front, back and side views. If your proposed house is to be supplied by a kit-home manufacturer, they will usually supply the floor plans and elevations.

A number of copies of the application plans and drawings will need to be sent to the planning office. Once processed, the council will inform neighbours of your proposal and tell them where they can see the plans and how long they have to give their opinions – usually 21 days from receiving the letter.

The outcome of a planning application can go four ways: refusal, delegated, deferred or permission granted. *Refusal* is the worst that can happen. You will be given a decision notice with the reasons why permission was not forthcoming. From this point you can either give up, re-apply taking the points listed into consideration, or appeal.

If your application is *delegated*, it will be referred to a senior planning officer. The planning committee will have already come to a virtual conclusion over the application but for one reason or another cannot totally commit to it. From this point the senior planning officer will await the contentious point to be resolved before giving a final verdict.

As with a delegated decision, a contentious issue or the late arrival of certain documentation could hold up an application. However, if the committee wishes to make the final decision, rather than pass it on to a planning officer, the matter will be *deferred* until a later date.

If *permission is granted*, make sure you read any conditions carefully. If you find these too strict, or are refused permission all together, you can appeal to the Secretary of State or re-apply with a different design.

The vagaries of planning departments can cause frustrations, but understanding what goes into a planning decision is vital for your success.

VAT

The labour and materials used in a self-build project are all free of VAT. Any VAT-registered contractors should not include VAT in their bills and, if you are managing your own site, you can claim back any VAT you pay within three months of the building being completed. Send in all invoices and receipts to Customs & Excise and the refund will be sent out within weeks.

10 Making extra money from your existing property

Increase your mortgage

The most obvious way to raise cash from your home is to take a lump sum by increasing your mortgage. This is also called a 'further advance.' You'll have to repay at your lender's standard variable rate, but as the cheapest personal loan rates are at least two or three per cent higher, you should save money.

A loan from a High Street bank costs more like 14 per cent APR. An additional loan is only worth having if your property is worth a lot more than the mortgage outstanding.

If you think you might want to take a slice of cash more than once, then think about a flexible or current account loan. With most flexible and current account plans you can take the money out of your account (up to a pre-set borrowing limit) without asking permission.

The independent statistics magazine *Moneyfacts* (*www.money-facts.co.uk*) has a selection of the best rates for flexible loans and personal loans.

Most lenders are amenable to giving extra loans, but it isn't widely publicised. All you need to do is phone your lender, ask what the process is, and you should be on your way.

You will have to pay for a current market valuation on your home (take this fee into account when weighing up the cost of an additional loan against a cheap personal loan). There may also be an arrangement fee.

You can choose to repay over a fixed period – either a shorter period of three or five years or as long as the mortgage – and the additional loan is kept separate from the rest of your mortgage borrowing.

Renovate your house

By planning any refurbishment or alterations carefully it is possible to increase your profit when you sell.

Firstly, there are a number of ways you can improve your property so that it saves you money. New building regulations mean homes are to become more energy efficient. Replacement windows should be double-glazed, boilers must be energy efficient, and conservatories and extensions better insulated. Improvements like these mean utility bills should be lower.

If your plans are more dramatic, remember the best way of substantially increasing the value of your home is by increasing its space and size. Adding an extra bedroom, an en suite bathroom, a large kitchen-diner, family room or conservatory will invariably increase the value of your home.

Always check if you need planning permission and building regulations approval. Keep all the relevant paperwork.

Equity release schemes

This kind of scheme is often of interest to older homeowners who are 'asset rich but cash poor.' Their house – usually with little or no mortgage on it – is mortgaged to raise a loan, which is used to purchase a pension, which is then used to supplement the borrower's income. The loan is also used to pay back interest on the sum borrowed. Be careful – this can be an expensive way to obtain extra money. If interest rates go up, the cost of servicing the loan would also rise and could take the majority of the income raised to pay back. Choose any scheme carefully and consider how flexible it is. Find a lender who operates under the Safe Home Income Plan scheme (SHIP) and always take advice from an independent advisor.

Location, location, location – cut!

You could make several hundred pounds a day if your home is used as a location for film or TV. All sorts of homes can appeal, and in some areas (especially in cities) you may find you get requests from location scouts posted through your door.

If you use an agency to market your home as a location, it will take a fee from any earnings you make, usually 10–15 per cent (plus VAT). For example, you can see what sorts of home are already on offer, and register online with the Location Partnership (*www.locationpartnership.com*) or Lavish Locations (*www.lavishlocations.co.uk*).

The BBC also runs a location register. You will be asked for photos and details of your home and will have to fill in a questionnaire (call 020 8225 9133).

Rent a room

Renting out a spare room is the most traditional way to make extra money. Many years ago the Government brought in incentives for this, under the Rent-a-Room scheme. If the income from your lodger is £4,250 or less, there's no tax to pay.

A Monday to Friday rental might be a good idea if you live in a city: people working away from home often need temporary lodging. All the better if your spare room has an en suite bathroom. Check out the going rate for room rentals in the local press.

Language schools are often in need of hosts for their students, although you may need to cook food and offer some pastoral care in exchange for the extra income. Then there are festivals and sporting events. Temporary accommodation is always needed, so you could move out for the duration and make some serious cash.

House swapping

This is increasingly popular especially as the Internet has enabled it to take off in a big way. It's not so much about making money from your property as more of a way of saving on holiday expenses. You simply swap homes with someone else for a holiday – or longer as some swaps last several months and would suit retired people looking for a long break.

Online directories list homeowners in other countries and details of their homes and available swapping dates. You can respond to these advertisements and/or advertise your own place and the places you'd like to visit. There's the additional benefit of leaving your house occupied while you are away, but you'll need to be relaxed about other people being in your home – and even driving your car.

Try www.homebase-hols.com or www.homexchange.com.

11 Improving your home

It may be stating the obvious, but if you don't like something about your property – change it. You don't have to live with someone else's decorating style or taste when you own your own home, so take advantage of the freedom and make it suit you.

Get rid of the swirly purple-patterned carpet, brighten up the kitchen, lose the dated avocado bathroom suite. Unless it's a major extension you're planning, you don't have to ask anyone's permission, it's your taste, your lifestyle and what you want that counts.

Of course, the amount of money you have will play a part in the creation of your dream home. If you have thousands of pounds, there's no doubt you can spend them. A top-of-the-range kitchen is in the £20,000-plus bracket. At the other end of the scale, £20 on a tin of white paint and some free hard work and enthusiasm – yours – smartens up a scruffy hallway.

If you can bear to, and it's practical, it's always a good idea to live in a house first before you plan any major changes. After a few weeks you know which rooms get the morning light and which benefit in the evening. If the sun shines so strongly into your bedroom it wakens you at dawn, then darker curtains are a must, and that will obviously affect any colour choice when it comes to decorating.

You will find out what items of furniture fit best into a particular space, which pieces you do really need to keep and which are now surplus to requirements. Put a couple of penny ads in the local paper and sell off what you don't want – put the cash back into your Dream Home Fund.

You've found your new home – but is it safe?

You've trawled round endless properties, found the house of your dreams, done your sums and made a decision. Did you know that your homebuyer's survey does not cover your electrics?

To protect yourself and your investment, it makes good sense to get an electrical survey carried out by an approved electrical contractor before you sign on the dotted line.

When a property is old or appears to have suspect wiring, many banks and building societies will ask for an electrical survey to be carried out before agreeing a mortgage.

The most common problem discovered during an electrical survey is a loose connection that can lead to fires or electric shocks. Around 10% of domestic fires are electrical, a third are directly due to old or faulty wiring. This equates to over 2,000 electric shock accidents and 9,300 electrical fires in homes every year.

An electrical survey is quick and easy to arrange

Getting a periodic inspection done is simple to arrange and to carry out. The first step is to find an electrician – search the NICEIC register on **www.niceic.org.uk** or call freephone **0800 328 7396**.

Your safety is our business.

You've found your ideal new home, and the survey is good. Now you can start arranging the moving date, and planning the design and decor.

But are you sure your survey has covered all the vital areas? It may come as a surprise to you, but most building surveys do not cover the electrical wiring and installation in anything more than a superficial fashion. Amazingly, this could mean that your new home actually needs rewiring, but you may not find this out until you've spent large amounts of time and money on decorating.

We would strongly advise you to arrange for an NICEIC-approved electrician to come along and do what we call a 'Periodic Inspection'. He'll inspect the condition of your wiring against the national safety standard, and recommend any work that needs to be carried out.

Visit our website, call us on 0800 328 7396 or e-mail us on marketing@niceic.org.uk for details of approved local electricians. You'll be glad you did.

www.niceic.org.uk

National Inspection Council for Electrical Installation Contracting

The basics

Don't do even the simplest job until you've had a chance to really think about the basics. What's the point of putting a set of shelves up on an internal wall when putting them in the alcoves would provide some cheap soundproofing from next-door's children? And no good will come of ripping out those old cupboards if a) they cover a spaghetti junction of pipes and b) you need the storage.

Look at the layout of the house. Is the best use being made of the space? Is that small room, which barely fits a single bed, not better fitted out with a desk and chair and used as a study?

Should the utility room be downstairs? What's the point of carrying clothes downstairs to be washed and ironed and then up again? Can't you move the room and have more living space on the ground floor?

Would knocking down an internal wall bring a lot more light into a room, or is it better to have a larger kitchen-diner than a separate kitchen and under-used dining room?

Kitchens and bathrooms are the two rooms that can cause problems. They cost a lot of money to replace and, perhaps because they are the most used rooms in the house, it can be very difficult to decide what is the best way forward. This is when it's essential to ask for expert advice. If you want a power shower, you need to find out about the water pressure. Before you buy that trendy and expensive cooker, you need to find out if the extractor fan can be fitted on an inside wall.

When you first move in:

▌ Check that any smoke alarms work – if there aren't any, fit at least two. Install fire extinguishers.

▌ Find the fuse box and the stopcock. Figure out how to work the central heating and programme it to suit you.

▌ Check with the seller that you have all the keys and change the outer locks if the property has been rented out.

▌ Ask your gas or electricity suppliers to send round an electrician, central-heating engineer or plumber to check out the wiring and plumbing system.

▌ Check the garden for security and make sure there's nothing around likely to injure you or children.

▌ Do a 'snag' list of all the minor jobs. Broken hinges, cracked windows, leaking taps. If you can't fix them yourself, find a handyman. If you are new to the area, ask your neighbour for a recommendation. Otherwise look in the small ads of the local paper or on the notice board of nearest Post Office, newsagent, church or café.

Major renovations

If you want to build an extension, add a conservatory, or do a loft conversion, then the advice of an architect or experienced builder, is a must.

You may think such a large building project would be too expensive or too much trouble, and moving into a new home would be a better idea. But extending upwards or outwards is much, much cheaper than estate agents' commission, stamp duty, removal costs and legal fees.

Stamp duty, in particular, is a killer. Payable by the buyer, it's a tax on already taxed income, and at one per cent for properties under £250,000, moving up to three per cent for properties over that figure but under £500,000, it can amount to a bill of thousands of pounds for simply changing your address.

So as good conversions always add value to your home and you will recoup your investment when you sell, you may want to hand a cheque over to the builder rather than the Chancellor of the Exchequer – you stand more chance of getting a return on your investment.

Beware though, not every addition will add value. Spending a fortune landscaping the garden will turn it into a nice place to

AVOID THE COWBOYS AND PROTECT YOUR INVESTMENT

By Paul Kendrick, Marketing Director, National Federation of Builders

Prospective buyers are savvier than ever when it comes to investing in property.

That's why it's crucial people get professional help when carrying our large home improvement projects designed to add value.

Poor standards of workmanship can seriously affect the eventual resale price and put off some buyers all together, leaving the vendor with a smaller-than-expected return on their investment.

A professional contractor may cost more than a cash-in-hand builder, buy why place one of your biggest assets in the hands of a cowboy?

One of the most common pitfalls for a homeowner is the cash-in-deal. By law, builders can only waive VAT if their annual turnover is below £56,000. Rogue traders operating above this threshold often tempt consumers with VAT-free deals and, with the current rate at 17.5 per cent, it's hardly surprising so many succumb.

But the end result is often poor quality work, which will only give potential buyers ammunition to negotiate down on price.

Homeowners should also seriously consider taking out a warranty to cover any building work done on the property. This will give prospective buyers the peace of mind that you've had a quality job done and that any resulting defects will be covered under a guarantee.

People often get caught out by the cowboys because they don't ask the right questions or fail to take sufficient time to look for reputable builders. Armed with the right information, you're much more likely to get the hassle-free results you deserve.

The vast majority of builders are professional, trustworthy and committed to getting the job done right.

The National Federation of Builders can advise you on how to source a reputable, quality builder and work with them to get the best results. For more details, go to **www.builders.org.uk**

Renovating or improving?

It's worth getting the right building company!

The National Federation of Builders is the industry's longest established trade association with almost 3,000 building and contracting companies as members.

To join the Federation, building companies must satisfy what we believe to be the most stringent entrance criteria for any building trade association. They must provide at least eight references from accountants, previous clients, suppliers and professionals such as architects and surveyors. The company must also be properly VAT registered (if applicable) and CITB-registered.

All references are checked and if satisfactory, applications are then put before a panel of existing members who are local to the potential new member for assessment.

Every potential new member is also visited on site before they are accepted.

The Federation also operates a Code of Conduct and a full complaints procedure, which involves a mediation and arbitration service.

Once accepted as a member, the building company can offer the 'Benchmark Plan' - an insurance-backed guarantee scheme which pays out the cost of correcting any building work defects for periods up to 20 years. This guarantee stays with the property so future purchasers of your property also get the benefit of your wise decision.

The National Federation of Builders has some of the country's best building companies as members. They have passed a rigorous entrance procedure, not merely a 'rubber stamp' application process. This is your assurance that when you deal with one of our members you are dealing with quality.

To find a member company near you, browse to our website www.builders.org.uk or contact our regional office nearest to you.

National
Federation of
Builders

Corporate Affiliate
of the Trading
Standards Institute

Construction
Confederation
Member

National Office, Construction House,
56-64 Leonard Street, London, EC2A 4JX.
Tel 020 7608 5150   Fax 020 7608 5151
www.builders.org.uk   info@builders.org.uk

The NFB has a network of regional offices across England and Wales - each one can provide a list of reputable, professional companies in your local area.

Eastern Business Centre
4 Archers Court
Stukeley Road
Huntingdon
Cambridgeshire PE29 6XG
Tel: 01480 420960
Fax: 01480 420969

North East Business Centre
Mount View
Standard Way
North Allerton
DL6 2YD
Tel: 01609 767320
Fax: 01609 737330

Southern Business Centre
Unit 12 Westlinks
Tollgate
Chandlers Ford
Eastleigh
Hants SO53 3TG
Tel: 02380 610050
Fax: 02380 651625

Western Business Centre
Richmond Court
Emperor Way
Exeter Business Park
Devon EX1 3QS
Tel: 01392 441090
Fax: 01392 441099

Midlands Business Centre
Kings Newton Hall
Melbourne
Derbyshire
DE73 1BX
Tel: 01332 865084
Fax: 01332 863236

North West Business Centre
3/5 Rough Hey Road
Grimsargh
Preston
PR2 5AR
Tel: 01772 693100
Fax: 01772 693101

Wales Business Centre
Ty Ffederasiwn
66 Cardiff Road
Glan-Y-Llyn
Taffs Well
CF15 7YA
Tel: 02920 815220
Fax: 02920 815221

enjoy a gin and tonic, but it won't add a cent to the price. Stone cladding, pillared porches and fitting modern windows into old properties are more likely to detract than add value. And gyms, hot tubs, swimming pools and bars in the sitting room are more likely to turn people off than attract them.

Good improvements and additions include:

- garage;
- an open-plan kitchen-diner;
- off road parking;
- extra lavatory;
- ensuite bathroom;
- good quality double-glazing;
- decent loft and cavity-wall insulation.

Improving your home, whether for yourself and family to live in or to make it easier to sell, can be a fraught process as mistakes can be costly to put right. But if you get expert advice, collect estimates for any work, have a good idea of what you want and, most importantly, take your time, you will find the challenge of it fun and satisfying.

Hallways

The first impression of your home should be welcoming. If the passageway is dark, choose a lighter shade of paint, install a couple of bright bulbs in the lights and hang a couple of carefully placed mirrors to reflect the light. Paint the radiator the same colour as the wall or hide it with a smart cover. Consider what would be the right kind of flooring. Wood or tiles are usually best for such a high traffic area. If you want a carpet ask at the showroom for a hard-wearing type, woven to withstand the wear and tear of football boots, trainers, wellingtons, work boots and

As heat rises with undertile heating, so does the value of your property

Long the choice of the designer cognoscenti, undertile heating is now making it big time as UK homeowners catch on to its many advantages. Fears of cold tiles can now be a thing of the past.

Market leading product, Warmup, creates an effective, efficient (10-15% more energy efficient than other forms of electric heating), and luxurious heating system for houses. The Undertile Heater is typically used in kitchens, bathrooms, conservatories and hallways, and in extensions and refurbishment projects.

Instead of relying on old carpets and traditional looking radiators to heat a home, undertile heating provides a very contemporary alternative – and one that works at creating a healthier home, by reducing dust mites. This is fantastic news for families with sufferers of allergies and asthma.

The Warmup Undertile Heater has been designed as a DIY product to be supplied in the form of a kit in three sizes. A thermostat, which includes a built-in timer, regulates the floor temperature. Warmup has significant design advantages over known competitive products. The heaters are very competitively priced, retailing from £163.99 including programmable thermostat and VAT. A typical sized bathroom will often cost less than £200 to heat when installing Warmup.

While undertile heating will definitely improve your home, it will also impress potential buyers when you come to sell your property. They do not have to worry about inheriting and having to replace old, dirty carpets – they know they will be moving into a home with clean flooring and one that is easy to maintain!

This undertile heating is easy to install – all neatly packaged in one box, simply buy off the shelf and install within 2-3 hours (a competent electrician will need to wire the heater to the mains). Thin and safe – Warmup features an advanced 2mm wire design taped down onto your existing floor (it's so thin it does not effect floor levels) then simply cover with tiles.

For more information contact
Warmup on 0845 345 2288

A simple way to add value to your property

Ideal for bathrooms, kitchens & conservatories

...at the floor with Primer

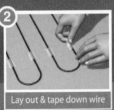
② Lay out & tape down wire

③ Connect Thermostat

④ Tile over Warmup Heater

Now beautifully warm tiled floors can be a reality

Warmup Plc   T 0845 3452288   F 0845 3452299   www.warmup.co.uk

gardening shoes. If there's space for a coat cupboard and other clutter, fit one, if not buy strong wall hooks and perhaps a shoe rack to keep everything tidy.

The sitting room

One person's good taste is another's example of 'naffness'. But you can't decorate for others, it's important that you live in a place that's comfortable and suits you and the way you live. It helps though if you don't have to do a complete makeover when you come to sell. Here's a basic guideline to help you overcome any pitfalls.

Focus on the space. Visualise the room as you want it. Think about where you will put electrical appliances like the CD player, the TV and lamps because all the wiring and cabling should be done before any decorating. The same goes for radiators. If you are installing a new central heating system, plan carefully to put the radiators in the most convenient places. Also, it's worth considering fitting under-floor heating. It's not so expensive anymore, is reasonable to run and is much more convenient when you come to place the furniture.

Remember that rooms always look smaller when empty so think about the sizes of furniture and fixtures carefully. A useful interior designer tip is always to buy a size larger than you think you need. So choose a larger lampshade, a bigger chair, and a chunkier coffee table.

Lots of owners 'knock through' from the sitting room into the dining room. This gives more space and perhaps more light. But you do lose a room. So if one person wants to watch the TV, and the other listen to music or use the telephone, it can be difficult. The installation of a door or double doors that can be closed for different activities to take place means more flexibility. Think carefully about combining rooms. Making a tiny kitchen into a much larger cooking and eating space by knocking through into the dining room is a popular idea. But making one bigger bedroom from two is not a good idea.

Safe as....

Choosing a new conservatory or replacement windows but don't know who to trust?

Every GGF member must work within our Code of Good Practice. Everyone that installs conservatories, windows and doors is also registered with FENSA to simplify working within the new Building Regulations. We offer a scheme to secure your deposit and even an arbitration and conciliation service if a problem can't be solved by other means.

So why not visit our home –www.ggf.org.uk– to find out why looking for the GGF logo helps you to rest easy in your home.

It can even help you to choose your installer with complete lists of members of our two specialist groups, the Conservatory Association and the Window and Door Group.

Glass and Glazing Federation

Glass and Glazing Federation 44-48 Borough High Street, London SE1 1XB, **Tel:** 0870 042 4255 **Fax:** 0870 042 4266
e-mail: info@ggf.org.uk **website:** www.ggf.org.uk

Give your home kerbside appeal

Windows and Doors – what you need to know

Windows are the first thing people see when they visit your house, so it's no surprise to learn that badly fitted windows can affect the value of your home. Your best bet is to choose a member of the Glass and Glazing Federation (GGF).

Especially as all replacement glazing now comes under Building Regulations Control.

This means that if you want to replace your windows, those new windows will have to be energy efficient. The reason for this is the Government's drive to ensure we, like the rest of the world, pollute the atmosphere as little as possible.

If in the future you then decide to sell your property, the purchaser's solicitors, when undertaking the necessary search, will ask for evidence that any replacement windows installed after April 2002 comply with the new Regulations.

You can prove that your windows comply in two ways:-
1. a certificate showing that the work has been done by an installer who is registered under the FENSA Registration Scheme
   or
2. a certificate from the local authority saying that the installation has approval under the Building Regulations

If you want to ensure that you comply with these Regulations and that the company undertaking the work will do a good job, you should make sure that you use a Glass and Glazing Federation (GGF) member who is FENSA Registered.

Conservatories – let the light in!

Sunshine is a vital element in our lives. This is reflected in the popularity of holidays abroad in countries where temperatures are in the 90s and the sun is guaranteed. It is also apparent when people buy a new home. Recent surveys have indicated that home owners say the more light there is in their homes, the happier they feel.

The British craving for light is also indicated by the popularity of conservatories. During the Victorian and Edwardian periods, the conservatory was most often used as a winter garden, allowing plants to flourish all year round. These days, it tends to be used as extra living space, making the design specifications ever more important.

The majority of all conservatories built today are double glazed and allow the household to make year round use of their additional space and to appreciate the aesthetics and benefits provided by its glass walls.

As The Conservatory Association – a specialist division of the Glass and Glazing Federation – points out, conservatories can come in all shapes and sizes in both modern and traditional styles, but the one thing that unites them is glass. Glass enables us to sit in a conservatory even on a cold and blustery day, and bask in the sun.

What design?
Among the most popular designs are:

The Victorian
Characterised by a ridge with ornate cresting and multi faceted bay end – usually either 3 or 5 facets.

The Edwardian
Typically this has a square end which makes good use of space, and a pitched roof.

Lean-to
Great for both big and small awkward spaces like corners.

When you choose a GGF Member, you can be assured that they:

1. Will comply with the new Building Regulations (relating to windows) and ensure you get the appropriate certificate via the Fenestration Self Assessment Scheme (FENSA).

2. Will have been in business for at least three years.

3. Have all been vetted to ensure they provide a quality service, the vetting procedure includes taking up references, looking at their accounts and site visits.

4. Work to the Federation's Code of Good Practice and technical guidelines.

In addition the GGF will provide you with:

1. A free conciliation service – should you and a Member company not see eye to eye over work carried out.
2. Protection for your deposit – the GGF Deposit Indemnity Scheme is backed by Norwich Union and safeguards deposits up to £3,000 or 25% of the contract price, whichever is lower.
3. A Customer Charter.

Contact us on: **0870 042 4255** for a list of members in your area or see **www.ggf.org.uk**

"Location. Location. Location."

Once heralded as the top three influential factors in the buying and selling of a home, 'location' is now having to share its places on the podium. Increasingly specification and brand selection are seen as persuasive ingredients when it comes to buying or selling a property. Today's purchaser understands that the cost of refurbishing a bathroom runs to thousands and a kitchen to tens of thousands and they will often bear that in mind when making an offer on a property. The discerning seller will ensure that they maximise the 'benefits' of their particular property by installing internationally identifiable brands such as Villeroy & Boch and SieMatic. Recognised as being of the highest calibre, designed to last and look good for many years, they represent excellent value for money. Just as people aspire to a Mercedes, Gucci or Prada, these products are desired by those who appreciate excellence in design and purity of purpose. They know that a SieMatic kitchen or Villeroy & Boch bathroom will not only impress their guests but will also provide them with a luxurious, yet robust environment to work or relax in. Obviously with products of such sophistication it is essential that the planning and installation is undertaken by an equally proficient team. That is why they are only available through specialist outlets that will be able to offer professional advice and produce a 3-dimensional 'virtual reality' model, allowing the customer to visualise the finished room prior to order.

Flooring and carpets

Flooring is all-important for comfort and warmth. If you decide on wooden flooring, you may need new floorboards or can sand and varnish the originals. If you have to fit new, think about installing a sound insulation strip underneath, especially if you live above others or in an upstairs room. Laminate flooring can look as good as the real thing and is cheap and easy to fit. If the floorboards are already in good shape, you can hire a sander and do at least a couple of rooms in one day.

If you think carpet is more comfortable, always buy the best you can afford – it's a false economy to skimp here – and, thinking ahead to selling, choose a plain rather than a patterned design.

Another interior design tip is to use the same carpet, tiles or wooden flooring throughout the house. This trick offers an illusion of space as spaces seem to flow seamlessly into one another and it's easier on the eye.

Original tiled or stone floors are worth keeping as a 'feature'.

Fireplaces

A fireplace is a real attraction and if it's original, all the better. They are a focal point in any room, and if you are fitting one you must make sure it is in keeping with the style of the property. There's a massive market out there now for all kinds for fireplaces – you don't even need a chimney.

Decorating

When it comes to decorating, less is more. Don't use lots of matching borders, wallpapers, curtains, cushions and throws. You can now even get matching wastepaper baskets in some designs! And don't paper all four walls with a very 'busy' theme. Put the expensive patterned paper on one wall and use a plainer design or plain paper on the others.

Pale colours can still be warming, yet they open a room up more and sell a property more quickly than dark colours. There's room for a little drama, particularly in the dining room, where the English seem to favour crimson.

White ceilings make them appear higher; dark colours lower them. And woodwork should be white or off-white. Painting walls white, however, won't necessarily make the room appear lighter. Use the mirror trick for that, and place a selection of table and standard lamps around the room to light up any dark corners.

Experimenting with different paint colours and effects is one of the cheapest ways to change a look and is easily changed if the colour doesn't look good.

Windows and doors

Replacing windows and doors can be expensive if you want to install double-glazing throughout or as cheap as chips if all you need to do is to re-hang a badly fitted and situated door. Of course, double-glazing is a major investment, but you usually get your money back when you come to sell and the savings on heating bills are worth making especially if you are in the property for a long time. If your home is in a conservation area, you must check before buying the property or installation if uPVC windows are acceptable.

When it comes to doors, think about the style and age of the property and the room. Is the room a little dark? Have a door with glass panels. Is the house an Edwardian Villa-style? Consider getting a couple of stained-glass doors. Is the room going to be used as a teenager's den? You'll need a heavy, well-fitted door to keep the noise of any music in.

Have a look at the layout of the room and see if the door is better opening on the other side. Does that give more room or better access?

Baumatic has become a name in kitchen appliances which not only offers an unmistakeable style, but also gives superb functionality at prices which won't break the bank.

This Baumatic philosophy applies across the full breadth of the range which encompasses: built in ovens; range cookers; slot in cookers; hobs; extractor hoods; microwaves; dishwashers; laundry; refrigeration and even sinks and taps.

There can be nothing worse than returning from a hard day's work and embarking on the housework, but Baumatic can help lift that burden from your shoulders. Most of the Baumatic portfolio is offered in stylish stainless steel. Not only does this finish look great, as any chef used to working in a professional kitchen will tell you, it is also incredibly hygienic and extremely easy to clean.

For some, however, a range cooker is just one of those kitchen 'must haves'. With some 15 models to choose from and prices as low as £700 we can make you feel just like Jamie Oliver standing in his professional kitchen!

With every inch designed for pure cooking power, Baumatic range cookers are available in 4 sizes, 70cm, 90cm, 100cm and 120cm, so there is bound to be a range that can fit into even the most compact kitchen. Our CK5 model, for example, offers all the benefits of a large range cooker with twin ovens, heavy duty cast iron pan stands, four burner gas hob and, of course, robust good looks, all in a tidy 70cm package.

But when size just isn't a factor, our Tennessee 120cm model offers all the features you could need. Finished in stylish stainless steel, this new model is a modern cooking icon. Standing in any kitchen its dimensions create an instant visual design statement.

Delve into the Baumatic portfolio ... we can turn your kitchen dreams into reality (**0118 933 6900, www.baumatic.com**)

Make-up for your kitchen

Americana Series

Mississippi   Arizona   Alabama   Indiana   Louisiana   Tennessee

The dining room

In many homes the dining room is the least used of any room in the house. 'Do you really need it?' should be the question you ask. It's all down to lifestyle and, practically, whether or not the kitchen is big enough to eat in. Many people now have the best of both worlds by knocking through, if possible, an adjoining wall and having one large kitchen-diner. That's all very well if you don't mind having a dinner party and your guests eat surrounded by evidence of the chaos that has gone into the cooking and the detritus of the meal at its end. But if you only have close friends and family around and you would rather put the room to better use as a second sitting room, or a children's playroom, you can because it's your house!

The kitchen

This is an important room and it's pretty crucial to get any renovation done properly as, when you do come to sell, a kitchen can make or break a sale, and to correct or change anything then can be expensive.

Sorting out a budget is the first thing to do. It doesn't matter what kind of kitchen you want, most styles can be found to suit any price range, but there's no point shooting off to a designer store if you don't have the money, nor traipsing off to a discount warehouse if you don't want a flatpack.

Designer kitchens

Financially the sky's the limit with a designer kitchen. Experienced cabinetmakers can design and fit a range of solid wood units complete with granite worktops and every appliance going. You pay for their craftsmanship – a £30,000 kitchen really should last you a lifetime; their professionalism – for that kind of

www.finebedding.co.uk

A duvet that bounces back...wash after wash!

At last a duvet that can be washed at home!

spundown
the duvet that loves to be washed

Whatever you get up to, a Spundown duvet can take it.

Our technologically advanced fibre filling compresses easily, so even a kingsize pops into a domestic washing machine. What's more the duvet can be washed at 60°C, the safe and clean way to eliminate dust mites. It's fresh thinking that means you can enjoy the feeling of a delightfully clean duvet whenever you like.

Call 0845 30 20 200 for your nearest stockist or visit House of Fraser, Beales Store Group and good linen shops everywhere.

THE **FINE BEDDING** Company

FRESH THINKING

SLEEP WELL, LIVE WELL!

We spend around a third of our lives asleep, and it's not time wasted! Good quality, regular sleep is essential to our continued physical and mental well being.

Just one night's disturbed sleep can leave us feeling irritable, unable to concentrate, generally rundown and less able to do even the most routine things. A recent Australian study shows that going without sleep can be as bad for driving as being over the legal alcohol limit.

So what is sleep?

Sleep is when the body gets busy doing essential maintenance work. During deep sleep, the body's blood cells, tissues and the immune system all benefit from 'in-house repairs'.

There are very important psychological benefits too. It's thought that dreaming helps the mind deal with the day's information. A brain 'in neutral' has the chance to sort things out, without the constant demands of running the daily consciousness getting in the way.

Sleep stoppers

Sleep therapists often recommend relaxation techniques and a little exercise during the day as basic aids to sleep. They'll also tell you to avoid coffee and tea, and eating large meals well before bedtime. And while alcohol seems to help you relax, it actually upsets your sleeping patterns, so you don't get the quality of sleep your body needs.

Bedroom basics

Of course, dealing with all these factors won't help if you're sleeping environment isn't right!

Quiet and calm are bedroom essentials, plus a temperature that's not too hot or cold – about 16°C is thought to be ideal.

But the most important thing to consider is your bed, particularly in terms of the mattress and bedding you choose. The ideal mattress is one that's supportive without being hard; when choosing a new one, make sure you lie on it for several minutes to ensure the mattress feels right. It makes sense to choose carefully, and buy the best you can afford.

The making of a beautiful bed

Comfort in bed is everything, and as we spend about a third of our life there, it's good to make bed as refreshing and pleasant a place to be as possible. Obviously we should regularly wash sheets and pillowcases, but what about the duvet and the pillows themselves?

With Spundown duvets from The Fine Bedding Company you can wash even the kingsize version without hassle, and keep your bed delightfully fresh as a result. That's because they've been designed to compress easily, to fit any domestic washing machine. It can be washed at 60°C – the temperature that kills dust mites.

Most pillows – even washable ones – tend to get lumpy, flat and uncomfortable over time. Contrastingly, Spundown washable pillows actually become plumper and more supportive with repeated washing and tumble drying. Their unique ball-cluster filling won't clump together to form lumps like the materials in other washable pillows. It too is washable at 60°C.

So improving your existing bedroom or even moving into a new home is a great time to replace your duvet and pillows – start a fresh and be able to keep it that way.

Breathe more easily

For a comfortable, refreshing night's sleep, its important that you let your body breathe. The Fine Bedding Company's Breathe Duvet and Pillow do just that. Made with unique blends of breathable fibre and fabric, that keep you cool when its hot and warm when its not, it is the ultimate in supreme comfort and softness. With the combination of soft fabric and filling, this breathable, luxurious duvet and pillow are simply irresistible!

Mild or occasional insomnia can often be solved by simple means, such as those covered here. But if you suffer from more serious sleeplessness, a visit to your GP is the best course of action.

money you should get good service; and their imagination – most good kitchen design ideas come from the top end of the market.

The kind of companies which offer these kind of kitchens can tailor-make a design to suit you, whether traditional or contemporary. They plan, create and install your choice and that includes any plumbing, re-wiring or decorating.

Planning your own contemporary kitchen

For those on a more modest budget, most DIY stores now offer a 3-D planning service. They won't come out to you, but if you take your measurements into the store, they input them into the computer and you can see what works in your kitchen plan. You might not be able to afford real granite or marble worktops but there are now so many stylish yet cheaper alternatives on offer: the room doesn't have to look as though you've cut corners. Just check that their cabinets are sturdy – remember the fitting counts here too – and that the hinges are good.

Kitchen appliances

You really don't have to spend a fortune to update a kitchen. Buy a trendy new kettle and toaster, paint the walls white, change the handles on the old units, replace the taps, lay a smart vinyl floor and install a couple of spotlights. You can do a lot for £300.

The second thing to do is to plan the layout. The all-important kitchen triangle is the cornerstone of the most conveniently designed kitchens. This works on the premise that the sink, fridge and cooker should all be close together and easily accessible from one to the other. If your fridge-freezer is the tall style, keep it at the end of the worktop, not in the middle. And the route between the sink and the cooker is the busiest so keep it free of clutter. Think about the plan logically; try and keep all the plumbing – sink, dishwasher and washing machine – in the same area. Put the crockery cupboards near the dishwasher. Don't put the oven too close to the fridge and keep the kettle near the cups, spoons and coffee and tea.

Experience Eloquence, the new definition of custom created sleeping pleasure. A dream bed born out of inspiration, it performs beyond mere functionality as a bed but it is a beautiful piece of contemporary design that can be modified to meet exact style requirements.

For further information contact 0870 742 9875 or visit www.restassured.co.uk for your nearest retailer.

by Rest Assured ELOQUENCE

Rest Assured

Sleep, or lack of it, is becoming more and more a prominent feature on the health agenda. Media reports are now regularly revealing to us scientific findings about how sleep effects us: Lack of sleep replicates the effects of the ageing process or reduces your IQ; Too much sleep is bad for you, yet too little means higher stress levels, increased mistakes and reduced concentration; Firmer beds aren't necessarily good for your back; Adults need seven to eight hours sleep a night, and you spend up to a third of your life sleeping.

With all these facts and figures being banded around on an almost weekly basis you may well be suffering from an attack of information overload! Add this to the evermore fervent pace at which society is currently moving, and you could be forgiven for allowing sleep to slip down your list of your priorities, especially when you are moving home! If this is the case, then it's very, very important to make the most of the sleep you do have so you don't become bogged down with one of the most stressful experiences you will encounter.

The first question you should ask yourself is are you sleeping on the right bed? The right bed is extremely important to our health and well being because our sleeping environment will affect the quality of our sleep – which in turn has a big affect on how well we feel, both physically and psychologically. A bed with the correct support, comfort and space ensures you wake less, move about less, are less disturbed by your partner and are less likely to wake up feeling tired, aching or any other of the media predicted states.

So, what is the right bed? First and foremost the right bed must give you the correct support and comfort. Individuals might also have to consider factors such as back pain, allergies, breathing problems, available budget, storage or space requirements, let alone style preferences they may have.

The right bed should also be no more than 8-10 years old. According to the guardians of all that is good with sleep, The Sleep Council, after 10 years a bed used regularly will have deteriorated by as much as 75% from its 'as new' condition. Nor should your bed ever be second hand if you can help it. Firstly it's not hygienic as we sweat as much as half to a pint of liquid a night. Secondly it's not healthy with the accumulation of all of the dust mites in your mattress, and most importantly of all, it will not provide you with the levels of support that you require having been moulded to someone else's sleeping habits.

So now you know what the right bed isn't, the problem becomes choosing from the mammoth variations that you have on offer to find the right bed.

There are many types of, and prices of beds from which to choose, each offering their own features and benefits. Firstly mattresses come with various types of internal spring unit – open coil, pocket sprung by which the mattress is made up of springs each individually encased in a pocket to provide individual comfort that moulds to your body such as those used by illustrious bed makers Rest Assured, or continuous springing. They can also come in a foam or latex material, filled with cotton or other fibres, and not forgetting the infamous waterbeds.

It doesn't end there either. There are many different base options too choose from – the original simple upholstered divans, to metal and wooden bedsteads or the all-singing, all-dancing adjustable beds. With consumers becoming ever more fashion conscious within their homes the bed is now firmly becoming one of their key style purchases. This has led to us seeing more and more contemporary stylings in the market place. Ranges such as 'Eloquence' from Rest Assured which features an industry first fully upholstered base and headboard, are now available in a choice of colours allowing you the chance to customise your bed to compliment your bedroom. They are positioned now not just as a bed, but as a fashionable piece of furniture that is a must-have item for any new home.

At the end of the day however, the choice is down to the individual. As was noted at the beginning of this article you will spend a third of your life in bed sleeping. With a mattress lasting an average of 10 years a £500 bed would equate to costing you only 7.3 pence per night for that 10-year period – not a bad investment if it provides you with a healthier lifestyle!

For further information please contact Rest Assured on:
Tel: **0870 7429875**
Web: **www.restassured.co.uk**
Email: **marketing@restassured.co.uk**

Range cookers

After the kitchen units, the most expensive purchase in the kitchen is likely to be the cooker. Most modern kitchens incorporate a separate hob and oven. And perhaps because of the popularity of the Aga, range cookers are becoming more common. Standing alongside the Aga or Rayburn cooker, is now an increasing selection of other range cookers, most of them adapted for a modern kitchen. They're not as big or complicated to use and look very attractive. But care needs to be taken if you are having a range cooker installed. Many of them need a chimney or have to be fitted on an outside wall where they can have a flue. They do take up more room than a conventional cooker and can look out of place within a run of very contemporary units, but they are sought after and, unfortunately, sometimes their prices reflect that.

Staircases and landings

Unless there's a natural divider between the hall, the stairs and the landing, I suggest painting the three areas the same colour, preferably using a bright shade. This keeps a narrow space, and usually quite a dark one, more open and light. Tough flooring is a must and, if you skimp, anywhere else, don't do it here. Buy the most hardwearing carpet or stair runner you can afford. It's a false economy to do anything else, as you will be replacing a worn and dirty carpet every two years. If you can stand the noise, varnished floorboards look great and are cheap and hard-wearing. Be warned – check you can get any new beds and wardrobes up the stairs before you buy them.

Storage

Roomy and well-made cupboards and shelves are a necessity. The average modern family has so much stuff and ample storage is

Architect: Fiona McLean

Corian+. Clean lines. Pure white.

Straight or curved, monochrome or colourful. With Corian+, you can express yourself, whichever way your tastes lean. Because Corian+ can be shaped into virtually any design you can imagine. Or mixed with any other material you can think of. With over 70 striking colours to choose from, your imagination can run free. With its non-porous surfaces and seamless joints, dirts and germs will have nowhere to hide. And because Corian+ is durable and renewable, the worksurface you create today will stay beautiful for years. (That should give you plenty of time to design a bathroom with Corian+.) Corian+ −for all the worksurfaces in your home.

Visit us on www.corian.co.uk or call
800/962116 (UK), 1800/553252 (IRL).

Kitchen Countertops as part of Designer Kitchens

'The countertop is the most important element in a kitchen, and the kitchen is the most important room in the home.' Irrefutable!!!

Most builders would agree that the plot sells the house and the kitchen makes it a home!!!!

We spend a large part of our lives in the kitchen and the countertop takes all we can throw at it.

We prepare food on it, drink from it, cook underneath it, wash up in it and the worktop is the most visible part of the kitchen.

It needs to be hygienic, easy to clean, look good and colour complement the kitchen (100) units, appliances and floors.

AND LASTLY the countertop material needs to give the designer the freedom to customise to consumers tastes and needs.

Kitchen Designers are always striving to maximise the functionality whilst maintaining the overall appeal of the kitchen.

The countertop or worktop must give the designer that ability to maximise their talents.

Up until recently Laminate tops have been the industry standard, giving a huge colour offer and a relatively long life. Consumers are continuing to spend more on their tops because their expectations of aesthetics, hygiene and longevity have grown.

Consumers have choices to make on the (200) type of finish, high gloss, matt, satin sheen etc.

Designers have a large selection of surfaces to choose from to tempt the adventurous consumer. Granite, solid surfaces, solid wood, slate, stainless steel are the most popular and growing considerably.

DuPont Surfaces now has two complementary surfaces to achieve all of the above.

Corian® achieves the highest satisfaction levels of all surfaces, research shows that over 90 % of purchasers would recommend Corian® to friends or relatives.

Corian® has a huge colour range, over 70 colours all of which are complemented by subtle 'shades of white' FULLY INTEGRATED sinks and bowls. (300) The integration of Corian® sinks in Corian® tops leaves a smooth, seamless joint and creates the ultimate in hygienic wet areas.

Corian® continues to allow designers to create sweeps and curves along the countertop; coving to allow a smooth transition from horizontal to vertical cladding, and round, oval dining areas attached to the countertop.

Accessories in Corian® makes customising tops and kitchens easier. Added features like Corian® knobs and handles, Taps from Avilion® with Corian® handles, Corian® Preparation Boards helps in adding that finishing touch to any design.

The new sensational material from DuPont is called Zodiaq®.

Made from the highest quality quartz, Zodiaq® is the most natural looking glossy surface, with unique strength, depth, clarity and radiance.

An exciting range of colours including deep reds and blues gives the design world a field (400) day to achieve stunning effects.

Exceptionally hard and cool to the touch, Zodiaq® is also non-porous, stain and heat resistant making it thoroughly hygienic and easy to maintain.

However the skills of kitchen designers these days are tested as many consumers would like to 'mix and match' several materials. Designers knowledge is also tested as they need to know ALL the features and benefits of each surface to guide consumers to the perfect countertop solution.

All these new materials are much more expensive than laminate but then again they have a lot more to offer.

Beautiful, hygienic, freedom in (500) design, easy to clean, are some of the words that can be used to justify spending larger proportions of customers budget on the countertop.

Corian® and Zodiaq® give 'value added' its true meaning as they complement not only the kitchen units, appliances and floor but their use can be expanded into other areas of the home, such as the dining area and conservatories.

There has never been a time like now when there is so much choice in design and materials to make kitchens the investment of a lifetime.

FreePhone No's: UK **0800 962116**
Ireland **1800 553252**

much prized. Most homes have wasted space that would be much better used if it was boxed-off into a cupboard or fitted with shelves and a sliding door.

Bedrooms

According to the people who collate those kind of useless facts and figures, we spend as much as a third of our lives in the bedroom. We might spend much of that time asleep, but that's precisely why we have to pay considerable attention to them.

How Many? After 'how much is it?' the second most asked question from a would-be buyer is 'how many bedrooms?' By adding a bedroom you will invariably add value, by removing one, the price will drop accordingly. That's the general rule of thumb, but there are exceptions. Two spacious and well-decorated rooms are a better bet than three tiny, cramped cells. And if one of the bedrooms is so small and out-of-proportion to the others, then turning it into an en suite bathroom may even up the price.

Beds and bedding

Because we spend so much of our lives in them, it's important to invest in the right kind of bed. This is a purchase that can't be rushed. Go to a large showroom and spend as long as it takes to find a comfortable and supportive mattress. Bed heads are a decorative feature and you can chop and change them for a couple of hundred pounds – or even make your own – but a decent mattress is a necessity and should last a decade. That's usually two house moves.

A bed is likely to be the largest piece of furniture in the room, there's no disguising it, so dress it up and flaunt it! Cheap bedding is one of the best bargains in the home improvement market. You can even buy quilts and duvet covers at supermarkets. Decide on how you want the room decorated and you will have no trouble finding bed linen to match. Or do it the other way round and use a stunning patchwork quilt or trendy, embroidered pillowcase as a starting point for your theme.

Bedroom furniture

As to the rest of the furniture, do you have freestanding pieces or do you want fitted wardrobes? The choice depends mainly on personal taste, but, obviously, built-in cupboards and drawers are more 'space-effective' in a smaller room and freestanding chests and armoires usually need a larger room to set them off.

Some furniture may have to do two jobs. If there's no space for a separate study, a dressing table may have to double as a desk, or think about those wardrobe-look-alikes which, when opened, show a computer with a pull-out keyboard shelf. And if you're short of storage, buy beds with drawers and build wardrobes to the ceiling to give space at the top. One eye-catching idea is to tear out the middle of a chimneybreast and fit it with extra shelves.

If there's only one bathroom, and the bedrooms have space, you might think about putting in a little vanity unit or sink and mirror. It cuts down on the queues for the bathroom each morning.

For a peaceful night's sleep, noise levels have to be low. This is where you might find double-glazing a necessity if your home is by a road or in the middle of a busy area. Also monitor noise from your neighbours. If only a slim partition wall divides your room from nextdoor's crying baby and those 3am feeds, think about losing a little space and fitting a secondary wall before you decorate.

Light is another factor. If the sun shines in too early, then curtain fabric and lining in a darker colour are going to help more than the currently fashionable muslin look. If you really need it, blackout material is easily bought, and many children's shops stock blinds and curtains already made up with it. Blinds always look nice and can be 'dressed' with ornamental curtains at the side to add interest. If you want to splash out and the room suits them, made-to-measure shutters look wonderful and are so flexible when it comes to privacy and light.

BUSHBOARD RE-LAUNCH FORMICA PRIMA COLLECTION – THE FULL CHOICE

The kitchen has become the focal entertainment and social room in many homes. Design in the kitchen is now vital to many who want to create just the right look to reflect their own personalities and style.

Bushboard's new Formica Prima range of worktop and splashback designs offer styles to suit all lifestyles, covering the whole spectrum of designs from natural wood and stone effects to mild steel, softer whiter tones to warmer red and copper effects. Bushboard's worktops and splashbacks are ideal for the instant kitchen makeover thanks to easy installation and a greater flexibility with a wider range of sizes and designs.

The new Formica Prima collection includes, for the first time, a choice of both 30mm and 40mm thickness, for 37 worktop designs in the standard finish colour range, a choice of 3 metre and 4 metre length options, and 10 worktop designs in the 3.6 metre gloss finish range. With 14 splashback designs in both gloss and standard finishes, including the modern design led 'Brushed Aluminium' design and the new 'Brushed Silver' design. Prices start from approx. £38 per metre for worktops and approx. £45 per metre for splashbacks.

For more information on the new range contact Bushboard on
01933 232 242 or visit **www.busboard.co.uk**

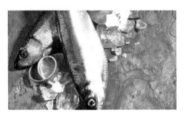

Bathrooms

Like kitchens, bathrooms are very important. A dirty, damp, depressing bathroom can put off even the most enthusiastic buyer or tenant. One of the reasons a would-be buyer may think again is the cost of fitting a new bathroom suite. Even the most dedicated DIY-er will probably have to get a plumber in here, and if there's any upgrading to be done in terms of electrics, damproofing or pumps for power showers, don't waste time trying to do it yourself. Get a couple of quotes and call in the experts.

Like Henry Ford said about his cars: 'Any colour as long as it's black.' Well, with bathrooms, it's got to be white. No avocado, no mushroom, no turquoise, at least not for the bath, sink and lavatory. White gives the impression of cleanliness and that's important in the smallest room in the house. It also appeals to more people, and one day you might want to sell.

Take a look at the layout of the room. If you're fitting a new suite it's cheaper and easier to keep the plumping pipes where they are, but check that everything is in the most convenient place. If the loo is the first thing you see, try to move it.

A plain bathroom suite is cheapest and doesn't date as quickly as a decorated one. And go for simple chrome fittings. You may like gold taps, but with all the other accessories – loo-roll holder, towel rails and soap dish – supposed to match, it can become a bit too garish.

If there's space for a walk-in shower, do fit one. If not then put one over the bath. This is the 21st century and a shower is an absolute necessity. And not one which offers just a pathetic trickle of lukewarm water. Ask your plumber if you need a pump to boost the water pressure. Always have a mixer tap on the bath even if there's a shower too.

If you are pressed for space, shop around for suites designed on a smaller scale for tiny areas. Even corner baths can now be found in a smaller size, and there's a whole range of 'thin' lavatories and sinks. If there isn't enough room for a radiator fitted from the floor, put it on the wall and it doubles up as a towel rail. Exactly how small is the room? Is it worth having a spacious shower room rather than a cramped bathroom? If there's another bath in the house, losing one and having a very trendy 'wet room' installed, won't cut the value. Ditto if you live in the kind of property, a flat perhaps, which is unlikely to be lived in by older people or children. But most estate agents will tell you that in an ordinary family home, they expect to see a bath – even if it is tiny.

There's also a debate raging about the number of loos a house should have. The typical newly built family home is given a downstairs lavatory, as well as an en suite bathroom and a family bathroom. That's three loos and seems plenty to me. If your property is an old one with just the traditional one bathroom, there's usually enough room to fit a second lavatory under the stairs. If you're considering a loft conversion, think about an extra bathroom or loo too. Don't add two bedrooms in the loft, putting more pressure on the one bathroom. Try two smaller rooms with a shower room, or one large master en suite.

Following through on the clean lines of a white bathroom suite, and particularly if there's little space, stick to tiles for decorating. Choose your colour and style and put them all the way up to the ceiling for height and space. Again, I'd keep the look simple and not too heavily patterned. If you have a nice large room, you could tile around the areas likely to get wet, then paint or wall-paper the rest, add a chair, a bookshelf and some pictures.

Storage is always at a premium in family bathrooms. Think about built in sink-units with cupboards and drawers under-neath. Or a run of bathroom cabinets down one wall. If you've had to box in any pipes, carry on the run and use it as shelving. If there's a nook, fit shelves or a door to make a cupboard.

Mirrors will make a space look larger, and fit downlighters as well as the overhead light. Some bathroom cabinets come supplied with lights inside and outside.

This is one area of the house where I don't recommend carpet. I know it's nice to step out onto after bath or shower, but you have to work so hard to keep it from getting damp and then mouldy that I don't think it's worth it. Tiles are easy to keep clean and dry.

Dunelm – Simply Value for Money, across the UK

With top brand products, excellent choice and first class service, Dunelm is the UK's largest independent specialist fabric and textile retailer.

Our stores are meticulously arranged in a 'colour blocked' layout to help customers easily co-ordinate their home interior requirements. Benefiting from wide aisles and zones dedicated to different areas of the home, our stores offer a huge selection of beds, bedding, quilts, pillows, curtains, cushions, throws, rugs, furniture, kitchenware, bathroom accessories, gifts and lighting. Each store houses a huge choice of textiles and soft furnishings from Dunelm's own brand to household brand names. For the more creative of us, Dunelm even stock over 1,200 fabrics sold by the metre.

Popular television programmes like *Changing Rooms* and *Home Front* have fired the imagination of homeowners everywhere, but people don't have to spend huge amounts of money or need a degree in interior design to make a real and positive difference to their home. Popular with all members of the family, Dunelm offers something for everyone.

So, whether you are looking to liven up your lounge, brighten your bathroom or put a fresh breeze in to your bedroom, Dunelm will provide thousands of soft furnishing products from which to choose.

Dunelm, originally based in Leicester has proved successful in over 50 towns and cities across the UK with their blend of products to suit all budgets. There is a comprehensive fabrics and haberdashery department with off the peg or made to measure curtains complete with an extensive range of fabric in every hue and pattern. With a warm and friendly welcome from professional advisors, customers are invited to visit their local Dunelm store and experience for themselves why Dunelm are 'Simply Value for Money'.

They can be cold underfoot but if you fit underfloor central heating there's no problem. Vinyl flooring is super. It's hard-wearing, easily dried and there's a huge choice of styles and colours. If you prefer bare floorboards, they're going to need an extra couple of coats of yacht varnish to make them waterproof.

The roof

You should have had a structural survey done when you bought the property and that would have given you a general description of the construction, the materials used and the condition of the timberwork, cladding, tiles, gutters and any insulation. You wouldn't have bought the property if there had been any major problems but, remember, prevention is better than cure and now you're the owner, any expense in the future will come out of your pocket. So do check regularly for any signs of trouble. Check to see the gutters aren't blocked by leaves or dirt – usually the cause of damp soaking through the walls. Mesh guards will prevent leaves being washed down pipes. Look out for any loose or missing tiles, or if the chimney needs to be repointed and that the TV aerial is securely attached.

Outside

The garden

The garden should be an extension of your living space, and no matter how small it is, any outside space is a value-added bonus when it comes to selling. You don't have to be Alan Titchmarsh to make any plot, whatever its size, a pretty and peaceful place to enjoy a glass of wine in the sunshine. Buy a lawnmower – they're as cheap as £30 – and a decent outdoor, hard brush for the paths.

After a weeding session, cover the ground with weed suppressing material and top that with bark chippings or gravel –

no more weeds and a tidy bed. You may not be a natural gardener, but it doesn't take long to maintain a garden to a standard you don't mind sitting in. It has to be said though, that a garden left to run wild and overgrown, or a patio or terrace neglected and weed-covered, is going to detract from the appeal of your property.

Gates and fences

Fit a decent garden gate, either in wood if you like the picket fence look, or iron. Remember that decent gates – front and back – are also security features. Repair fences, paint an old shed, and plant up a few pots with bright flowers.

Other security features

Most new windows and doors have to conform to regulations that aim to improve household security and therefore have proper locks. If you've replaced windows and doors and already have new double glazing, then, alongside a burglar alarm and decent outside lighting, that's probably as much as you will want. If you are not replacing windows and doors, fitting tough locks and latches is a necessity. It is probably a condition of your insurance policy. For those who want a higher level of security, a security expert or a visit from the police, will point you in the right direction. Proximity alarms, floodlighting and sensors are all easily available. If you work from home and have reason to keep large sums of money there, think about having a hidden safe set into the floor or a 'secret' cupboard built for valuables.

STEPPING UP THE TEMPO ON DESIGNER WARMTH

Myson, the first name in designer warmth, has unveiled a stunning new range of individually handcrafted decorative radiators.

Created with the modern home in mind, the Tempo range is bold, modern, elegant and functional, completely redefining the concept of heating throughout the home.

As the emphasis shifts towards quality design in the household, we are increasingly choosing products based more on materials, craftsmanship and performance. The tempo range is designed to meet these more demanding criteria, and create new opportunities for designer warmth in any room in the house.

Ten vertical heating tubes on either side of a full-length mirror makes Cantata (see photo) a high design-led wall-mounted bathroom radiator with a very small footprint in relation to its maximum heat output.

Cantata design taken from the new Tempo range

Inclusion of a mirror makes this design especially attractive in hallways and bedrooms as well as bathrooms. Both versions, either symmetrical or asymmetrical, are 600 mm wide with an option of including one or more hanging rails.

Other details: available in two heights (1190 and 1800 mm); finished in chrome, brushed or bright nickel, 22 carat gold, white or colour.

Ophelia – The High Quality Solid Surface Solution That Adapts to Your Personal Space

Orama, the leading independent manufacturer of worksurfaces and associated decorative products, has developed a new solid surface made from the finest materials, Ophelia. The end result is a surface system that combines both pleasing aesthetics and durability. Ophelia surfaces have been designed for living, thereby making the most out of any environment. Space is optimised affording a feeling of freedom.

Ophelia is a cast composite engineered construction for enhanced performance. The specialist materials are chemically linked into one structure, which is in turn bonded onto a sealed moisture resistant board so that it can be easily installed and fastened into place.

This new product offers a cost-effective surface solution combining resistance and flexibility with a modern designer granite matt finish. This ensures that it retains an overall natural look and feel coupled with a touch of modernity. The surface is therefore an ideal upgrade to laminates and loses none of the appeal currently emerging, as worksurfaces are undergoing complete transformation and renewal. Not only is it stain-resistant, but it offers virtually inconspicuous joints.

Ophelia is easy to install and provides the ideal surface solution for environments where the hazards of moisture and heavy wear may be of concern. The smooth matt surface is easy to clean and maintain so long as basic simple wear and tear precautions are followed. Superficial scratches can be removed with a buffing pad. This ensures that the surface is hygienic, repairable and easy to care for. In addition, Ophelia is heat resistant up to 185°C.

Ophelia can be readily formed into a number of shapes. This new solid surface system can be cut to suit requirements. For example, the surface accepts all inset and sit on type sinks. Benefiting from a standard 28mm depth, this product is available in customised dimensions – a 600 mm x 3000 mm run and a 900 mm x 2000 mm run – thereby reducing excess material waste.

Orama offers high quality durable decorative panels and worksurfaces. Established for many years, Orama holds ISO 9001 certification and the Furniture Industry Research Association Gold Award for product performance. They are also a corporate member of the KBSA (Kitchen Bathroom Bedroom Specialist Association). All Orama's chipboard and solid timber products are sourced from 'responsibly managed' forests.

For more information about Orama worksurfaces, please contact Orama directly on: **01773 520560** or visit the website on www.orama.co.uk Please send all leads from this editorial FAO: Sarah Brook on **sbrook@orama.co.uk**

Kitchen Worksurfaces that are designed for living

Ophelia is a new range of high quality solid surface kitchen worksurface products that are made from the finest materials to deliver pleasing aesthetics and durability in use.

OPHELIA ADVANTAGES

- Modern designer look matt finish
- The look of granite in a solid surface
- Hard and non porous
- Virtually inconspicuous joints
- Easy care: easily maintained matt finish
- Available in 3 attractive designs

SAND

VANILLA

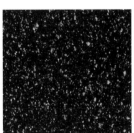
COAL

For more details on Ophelia or any Orama kitchen worksurface please contact 01773 520560.

Azalea Close, Clover Nook Industrial Estate, Somercotes, Derbyshire, DE55 4QX. Telephone:01773 520560, Fax:01773 520319
www.orama.co.uk, E-mail:enquiries@orama.co.uk

12 Buying abroad

Points to consider

First of all you need to decide what you want out of a property overseas. Is it mainly for holidays, for a retirement home, for rental income or capital appreciation?

Five years ago two-thirds of people looking for property abroad were buying for retirement. Now at least a quarter are buying for investment and, although investment buyers are generally in their 40s and 50s with some spare money to hand, there is an increasing number of younger people looking for alternatives to paying into a pension.

Buying property abroad is becoming more attractive as the buy-to-let market in the UK looks increasingly vulnerable, and as the proliferation of cheap flights in and out of local airports gives a wider choice of area to buy in.

Most Britons want to buy in Spain – other popular destinations include France, Florida, Portugal and even as far afield as South Africa.

When deciding where to buy, personal preference will be influential, particularly if the property is to be used as a holiday home for some of the year. But experts advise buyers to do their research first.

Visit the area, investigate the prices of local properties yourself and find out what other people are doing. The location will determine for how many weeks of the year the property is likely to be let. In Tenerife, with warm year-round weather, you can expect your house or apartment to be let for 45 weeks annually. In

Why travel with **hoverspeed**?

Hoverspeed is the leading fast ferry operator on the English Channel operating Seacats on two routes with the fastest sea crossings to France:
- Dover-Calais, up to 15 return sailings per day, crossing in around one hour
- Newhaven-Dieppe, up to 3 return sailings per day, crossing in around two hours

You'll notice the difference when you travel with Hoverspeed. That's why we've been welcoming back our customers for the past 21 years. We make sure that every step of the process is made as easy for you as possible from the time you make your reservation until you disembark. We understand that you want to experience a fast, comfortable and enjoyable service and that's why we focus on…

*hover*speed
- Quickest Channel crossings by sea
- Fast-track check-in at our exclusive terminals with no coaches or heavy goods vehicles to delay you
- Fast loading and unloading and easy motorway access in both the UK and France
- Save time travelling and spend more time at your destination!

*hover*style
- Sleek, wave-piercing Seacats
- Luxurious passenger areas with a choice of spacious seating, refreshments and shopping facilities
- Take in the sea air on the outer deck
- Airline-style, uniformed staff
- Upgrade to 1st for the ultimate pampering experience

*hover*service
- Regular sailings throughout the day
- Seacats carry up to 140 vehicles and 650 passengers
- Friendly, well-trained staff are always close by to help out
- At-seat service for refreshments and retail goods
- Shops packed full of all your favourite wines, beers, spirits, tobacco and more – all at great savings on the UK high street price
- 3 ways to book – phone, web or travel agent

Choose **hoverspeed** for your next journey to France…

frequent traveller? save 20%

If you travel 6 times a year or more with Hoverspeed, you can save an instant 20% off all publicly available vehicle and foot passenger fares. Its not often you get an offer this good.

For more information on free membership of Hoverspeed's Frequent User Scheme, call 0870 460 7171 or visit www.hoverspeed.com.

dovercalais **newhaven**dieppe *fast*

the mainland tourist areas – usually close to a big city – of France or Spain, 25 weeks is more likely, while in more out-of-the-way rural areas only around 12 weeks through the summer is achievable.

The property should be near an airport or other excellent transport links, be nearby some local attractions, look good in a photo and be cared for between lets. Do think about your market – families want gardens and pools for children to play in, not wrought-iron balconies with stunning views over steep drops.

Many agents will organise a research trip to the area for prospective buyers. British Homes Abroad, for example, which markets property in Florida, will arrange an apartment for buyers to stay in while looking and will refund the cost of the stay if a purchase is made through them.

In general, investors can expect annual rental income of about 7.5 per cent of the value of the property, after deducting all expenses and including the costs of a managing agent. These generally charge between 15 per cent and 20 per cent of rent. For those who decide not to employ an agent, the time and expense of finding tenants, paying bills, cleaning, marketing and maintenance must be considered.

Buyers have two options when raising money to finance the purchase of a property abroad. The easiest is to borrow against a UK property, not necessarily in sterling, although this requires adequate equity available to finance the overseas purchase.

The second option is to borrow abroad against the property, which avoids currency risk. But there are generally fewer deals available than in the UK and you must feel confident about negotiating in another country. British Mortgages Abroad is a company that offers mortgages for buying property abroad through First National and Abbey National.

The maximum loan to value is between 75 per cent and 85 per cent and mortgages are not offered on the strength of anticipated rental income.

Mortgage broker Charcol advises that, because a deposit will be required and the costs associated with buying will be between 10 and 15 per cent, buyers will need a cash sum of between 30 and 35 per cent of the purchase price. Overseas mortgage specialists, such as Conti Financial Services, can give detailed advice on specific markets.

As well as financial advice, buyers will need legal guidance, preferably from a lawyer with a knowledge of UK law as well as the law of the country where the property is to be bought. A buyer also needs to be on top of the tax implications of owning property abroad before making an investment decision.

Rental profit on property abroad will be taxed in the UK, even if the money is kept overseas or reinvested in the property. Certain expenditure is deductible from rent, particularly upkeep of the property, but not capital expenses. Foreign tax payable on the rental profits can be credited against UK tax.

Euro mortgages

Taking out a mortgage in another country can mean access to cheaper borrowing rates. But the levels differ widely across the Continent, and some markets are less competitive than the UK.

UK-based borrowers will also have to remember that they are taking on additional currency risk with a euro-denominated loan. The stability of the euro is constantly called into question and if the value of the euro rises against sterling, borrowing costs will increase.

The arrangements for conveyancing and legal requirements associated with buying a house abroad can vary from country to country. But there is a growing number of specialist mortgage brokers and advisers who can hold homebuyers' hands through the process.

Conti Financial Services, based in Hove, East Sussex, produces a series of fact sheets to help prospective customers. Some of this information can also be found on its website at www.conti-financial.com.

France

Variable rate mortgages are available at 3.7 per cent with higher fixed rates. A repayment mortgage generally requires a 15 per cent deposit, with a 20 per cent down-payment needed for an interest-only loan.

All mortgages need to be accompanied by a life assurance policy, and with some lenders these come free.

A survey or valuation is not compulsory and many lenders do not conduct them, so borrowers may wish to organise their own.

All borrowers in France will need a French bank account and will need to show the lender proof of income. This involves at least three months' payslips or three years of audited accounts for the self-employed.

French lenders do not take into account the value of any rental income when calculating the affordability of the mortgage. They also require that all your existing liabilities, including any other mortgage or rent payments, personal and bank loans, credit cards and divorce maintenance payments – together with your proposed French mortgage – must not exceed 40 per cent of your net monthly income.

Spain

Variable rates are currently available from around 3.98 per cent, but early redemption penalties apply in many cases. Homebuyers have to pay a minimum deposit of 20 per cent.

Borrowers need to show proof of income and Spanish lenders do not take into account rent on the property in deciding whether you can afford the mortgage. The affordability of the loan is based on existing liabilities, together with the requirement that your proposed Spanish mortgage should not exceed 35 per cent of your net monthly income.

Borrowers are warned that they must obtain title to the property – the *nota simple* – often before a lender can carry out a valuation. Buyers of new property must have it registered in their name and not that of the builder before the loan can be secured. If your house is under construction, Spanish banks will provide 'stage' financing in instalments, but only if it is registered in your name.

Fixed loans are available at 3.75 per cent for the first year with variable rates at 5.75 per cent. A deposit of 30 per cent is required and repayment mortgages only are offered.

Italy

Variable rates are on offer from 4.3 per cent with a minimum 20 per cent deposit. Repayment mortgages only are available and some discounted rates are available.

Borrowers need an Italian bank account and a tax code, which a lawyer will arrange. British homebuyers need to be aware that the Italian system is bureaucratic and can lead to delays in getting financing in place.

Portugal

Variable rates are at about 4 per cent, with a minimum deposit of 20 per cent. Some lenders are prepared to take into account rental income as well as salary and pension when calculating the level of loan on offer. A life policy is required when taking out a mortgage.

Eastern Europe

Some mortgage brokers are now turning to the EU's candidate countries as an investment opportunity for UK buyers. Countries such as Poland and the Czech Republic will join the EU in 2004 and some will place restrictions on purchases by overseas buyers. But some companies are finding ways round this – such as setting up a limited company in the country to buy the property.

13 Buying a home in Scotland

A different legal system

For anyone buying property in Scotland for the first time it is important to be aware of the correct way to go about it. This is particularly the case for anyone moving from England, as there are fundamental differences between the Scottish system and that operating 'South of the Border'.

Although the basics are the same, it is the timing of when the contract becomes legally binding that has led to two different approaches. It is important to understand that there is no second step in the Scottish procedure and that the contract can become legally binding at a relatively early stage, unlike in England where contracts are often exchanged towards the end of the process. In Scotland, they prefer not to wait until the removal men are at the door before exchanging contracts.

The contract takes the form of a series of letters known as missives, which are signed by the parties' solicitors. Once the offer has been accepted on all points, you have entered into a legally binding contract and neither party can withdraw without potentially being held liable for the consequent losses of the other party.

Accordingly, you should be careful and only put in an offer in Scottish legal form through your solicitor. If you offer in writing yourself and this is accepted you could end up being committed to buying a 'pig in a poke' – a well known Scots non-legal term!

BUYING IN SCOTLAND

There are several key differences between the Scottish and English systems of house sale and purchase. This is why anyone moving into or out of Scotland will require the services of two solicitors – one in each country.

This is because buyers or sellers in Scotland must use a solicitor qualified in Scots Law. If moving within Scotland, one solicitor will suffice.

Solicitors' Property Centres

In many parts of Scotland, the majority of property sales will be handled by solicitors, who also act as estate agents. There are Solicitors' Property Centres throughout the country, where you can access details of thousands of properties for sale. To find your nearest centre, visit www.sspc.co.uk

The largest property marketing organisations in Scotland is Edinburgh Solicitors Property Centre (ESPC), which at any given time has up to 4,000 properties on its books. It covers all of east central Scotland, with property showrooms in Edinburgh, Kirkcaldy, Dunfermline, Falkirk and Stirling.

Established in 1971, and with 265 solicitor members, ESPC is a well-known and respected authority on property marketing. In addition to its showrooms, its properties are marketed through the website (www.espc.com) and a weekly property guide *ESPChomepages,* which is available from banks, building societies, selected supermarkets and retail outlets and member solicitors across east central Scotland.

As well as the website and property guide, ESPC's services include: free property matching; mortgage advice; a solicitor referral service if you don't have a solicitor; and a 24-hour dial-a-schedule answering service, which lets you request property details by post if you don't have internet access.

For further information on buying a property in Scotland, call ESPC on **0131 624 8000** or visit www.sspc.co.uk for your nearest Solicitors' Property Centre.

Issued by ESPC(UK)Ltd
For further information contact:
Kate Gillespie/Simon Fairclough
t: 0131 624 8888   m: 07710 472731   e: marketing@espc.com

SOLICITORS SELL HOUSES

There's one sold every six minutes through ESPC!

If you're looking to buy or sell a property in east central Scotland, you'll want to visit one of ESPC's Property Centres.

With details of thousands of properties, our website and network of showrooms and solicitor firms have made us the market leader.

Whether you're looking for a property, a mortgage or advice on any aspect of your move, ESPC has the answer.

0131 624 8000   **www.espc.com**

ESPC
EDINBURGH SOLICITORS
PROPERTY CENTRE

Edinburgh   **Dunfermline**   **Falkirk**   **Kirkcaldy**   **Stirling**

The different legal systems have to be considered particularly carefully if you have a house to sell in England and you are relying on that sale to fund the purchase of a house in Scotland. You will require separate solicitors, and it is important that your English solicitor is aware of the need to progress the sale procedures as swiftly as possible.

Scottish solicitors

It may be tempting to think, 'surely I don't need another solicitor – it's just a case of filling in a form'. Certainly with Land Registration, the conveyancing part of the process is more straightforward but most properties in the Borders are still not registered. Even where the property has been registered, there are still aspects of the transaction that require a careful eye. Solicitors are used to dealing with buying properties. The length of a standard Scottish offer is built on the experience of problems that, to a lay person, would not be obvious. If you are borrowing from a bank or a building society, they will certainly require the security work to be done by a solicitor – so why take on any unnecessary worry?

You might think that, now we are all in the single market place in Europe, your solicitor in England should be able to deal with the purchase – but he can't. Scotland has its own separate and distinct legal system. The legal environment is different and you will require a Scottish solicitor to look after your interests. Although some agents do sell houses on either side of the border, the estate agency part of the selling process should not be confused with conveyancing. You will still need a Scottish solicitor.

The costs

As property prices have risen the Government has taken a bigger slice of the cake in terms of indirect taxes. Stamp duty is currently 1 per cent of purchases between £60,000 and £250,000, 3 per cent on properties between £250,000 and £500,000 and 4 per cent above that. This is payable on the whole of the price, so a purchase at £450,000 would involve a stamp duty bill of £13,500. On top of that there is the cost of registering the title, which, again, is charged on a sliding scale increasing with the value of the property.

If you ask a solicitor for a comprehensive breakdown, you might be pleasantly surprised at how the fee element compares. At the end of the day you will need a bottom-line figure for budgeting purposes. Any solicitor should be prepared to give you an indication of the likely costs at the outset of the transaction.

The asking price

In Scotland properties are usually marketed on an 'offers over' basis which is just an indication of the price that the seller is being advised to look for and does not mean that a lower offer would be refused. It will depend on the competition and various other factors. For example, if the property has been on the market for a while and there are no competing purchasers, it might be worthwhile offering less than the asking price and making your offer subject to a satisfactory survey.

An offer 'subject to survey' is less attractive to the seller as it puts the buyer in control, so if your offer were acceptable in principle, a seller would generally respond by setting a time limit for the survey to be done. This might be appropriate where you have a limited budget or there are particular circumstances but as a rule it is advisable to get a survey, or at least a valuation, first. An offer 'subject to survey' is unlikely to be accepted at a closing date unless it is considerably higher than the other offers.

Ready cash?

Do you need to have the cash available on the day you offer? Not strictly – you will only need the funds for the purchase at the settlement date – ie the date specified in your offer, which can be weeks but is more usually months ahead. This is when you will pay the price in exchange for getting entry to the property.

If you have a house to sell, particularly if the house is in England where a different system applies, you must be confident that the funds will be available or be prepared to take on bridging finance. If there is substantial equity in your home, some banks will still agree open-ended bridging and, with interest rates as low as they are at present, it might be worth taking a 'minimal risk' to secure the property of your dreams. However, you should be careful and get the bank to put any bridging facility in writing.

Noting interest

If you don't want to miss out on a chance to offer, you should ask the selling agents to note your interest. In that way, if another party offers, you may be given an opportunity to submit a competing formal offer, in which case a closing date may be fixed. However, the selling agents are not bound to do so and if an acceptable offer comes in, the property might be sold without it going to a closing date.

Closing date

If a closing date has been set and you have noted your interest, you will be invited to submit your offer by a specific date and time. This system has its critics, as you are in a blind bidding situation, but it generally means that the seller achieves the best price and, where there are a number of interested parties, it gives each an opportunity to submit an offer. The downside is that you will incur costs, particularly for a survey, which will be no further use to you if your offer is unsuccessful.

If a closing date for offers is fixed, you will need to have done all your homework before you are ready to offer. It is advisable to have a survey carried out, and your funding arrangements should

Maintaining Your Peace of Mind

How often is it that homeowners only pay heed to the basic maintenance of their property when a problem actually arises, or when they are preparing their most valuable asset for sale. However a properly maintained and secure property not only provides peace of mind and pleasure during your stay in the house, but is very likely to make a real difference when it comes to selling.

Whatever the timing or extent of the repairs do not be tempted to do maintenance on the cheap. There are regrettably still traders who will offer to do "cash in hand" deals but be aware that the offer that seems too good too be true usually is, a so-called bargain very often turning out to be a very expensive mistake.

It doesn't have to be like that of course, with reputable trade associations like Scottish Building having very strict criteria for membership covering workmanship, customer care, guarantees etc. In Scotland we also have the Construction Licensing Executive, an independent regulatory body for the construction trades which seeks to deliver real consumer protection and which has the involvement of Trading Standards and the Scottish Consumer Council among others.

So apart from seeking out a reputable contractor, what measures can you take to ensure that any job, large or small, goes as smoothly as possible? The following brief step-by-step guide should help both the customer and contractor to deliver a satisfactory project.

1. Step One
   What do I Want?
   Decide what work you want to be carried out, put this in writing and give a copy to any potential contractors so they fully understand what is expected of them.

2. Step Two
   Who Will Price the Work?
   When trying to decide upon the contractors you want to price your work, get referrals from family and friends who may have had work carried out recently, but do not forget to do your own investigative homework.

   Work your way through a vetting procedure – ask for help from the CLE or from the Trade Body whose members carry out the type of work you have in mind. Scottish Building is split into 19 Local Associations covering the length and breadth of Scotland, and they will be delighted to provide a list of registered contractors who operate in your area. Other bodies such as SNIPEF and SELECT can also provide member company names for the plumbing and electrical trades respectively.

3. Step Three

How Much Will the Job Cost?

Obtain written estimates. When approaching your potential contractors make sure *they* clearly know and understand what *you* want *them* to do. Make sure the estimates are in writing and fully detail all the work to be done, show the amount of VAT to be charged and detail the timescales involved. Also, check with the contractors the position you are in with relation to Planning Permission and Building Warrant Approval.

4. Step Four

What about References?

From your chosen list of contractors who are prepared to provide written estimates, ask for references and be sure to follow them up. For your own peace of mind ask each contractor for more than one reference and, with their permission, follow them up and ask their clients not only about the work that was carried out, but the level of service they received. It may even be an option to go and view some of their recently completed work or projects.

5. Step Five

What type of contract should there be?

Once you have considered all your options, a decision will have to be made as to which contractor you are going to use; always remember cheapest may not always be best.

An agreement and contract should be made between yourself and your chosen contractor – *in writing*.

The contract should cover all the work to be done, the date the work will start and finish, materials to be used, hours of working, warranties and insurances available and so on.

Scottish Building has its own Homeowner/Occupier Contract that is available free of charge and offers an easy to follow contract for homeowners. Scottish Building also has an extensive range of contract documents suitable for any contract large or small.

6. Step Six

   Is There a Guarantee?

   Prior to signing the contract check what type of Guarantee and Warranty
   Scheme your chosen contractor operates, make sure that it gives you the
   cover you need and want. Companies who are members of reputable
   Trade Associations should be able to offer a well-tried and tested form of
   warranty.

   Member companies of your Local Association of Scottish Building have
   available the BuildSeal Guarantee Scheme which is free of charge to
   members' customers and offers additional peace of mind as well as
   practical and/or financial assistance in the unlikely event that any
   problems should arise. All that is asked is you employ a Scottish Building
   member company and an approved Scottish Building Standard form of
   Contract is in place.

7. Step Seven

   What about Insurance?

   Before any work begins, ask to see the contractors' Certificates of
   Insurance. Also, check your own Home Insurance Policy as the work you
   are having done may affect your own insurance cover; your insurer may
   suggest you take out additional cover. It is important to remember the
   work will be carried out on *your* property and *you* must be sure that *you,
   your property* and the *public* are protected should anything untoward
   happen during the period when the work is being carried out.

8. Step Eight

   Keep a record of any changes

   During the contract be sure to record any changes to the works and
   ensure that the contractor confirms, in writing, any effect these may have
   on the value of the project. Extras requested by customers during the
   course of a typical project can add considerably to the original quotation
   for the work and it is in the interest of both parties that there are no
   "surprises" when it comes to payment on completion.

9. Step Nine

   How and When do I Pay?

   Payment is a vital part of any contract as you will be well aware!! Agree what you are going to pay and when, *in writing*, prior to any work commencing. Avoid paying any deposits before the work commences, deposits should only be made when specific or custom-made materials are needed. Only agree to stage payments if the contract is of longish duration, but make sure you are clear when these payments will be made and what work will be completed at that time.

To avoid any disputes with your nominated contractor always make sure that you have sufficient funds available to pay the contractor in accordance with the agreed payment schedule.

10. Step Ten
    Do I Pay Cheque or Cash?
    The "VAT Free" deal may not offer value for money. Within the Construction Industry there are many genuine companies who do not charge VAT simply because their annual turnover is less than £55,000 and do not need to register for VAT, but you must be sure if you are having any substantial work done that they are capable of carrying the size of project you have in mind.

    However, there are also those "contractors" who may offer not to charge VAT for payment in cash, and this is where the consumer must be very wary. A VAT-free deal could mean that the contractor is avoiding tax liabilities, which obviously means they may not be operating legitimately and could be a 'cowboy contractor' or a 'rogue trader'.

    If you do not have any payment receipt, what proof is there that the contractor actually did the work for you, and what happens if you find fault with the work in the future – will that company still be around to help you?

So there are ways to maintain your peace of mind as a homeowner or seller provided you follow simple steps designed to avoid the problems which cutting corners can lead to. Contact our Marketing Department to find out more or visit our website at **www.scottish-building.co.uk**

Bill Goodall
Federation Secretary
Scottish Building

18 November 2003

SCOTTISH BUILDING

be in place. Your solicitor can instruct a surveyor (and obtain quotes from specialist contractors should treatment for woodworm, damp, dry/wet rot etc, be indicated) and help you find a mortgage, either directly or through a broker.

Concluding missives

If your offer is successful, your solicitor and the seller's solicitor will then negotiate the 'missives', which are the formal letters passing between them dealing with the finer points of the contract that will finally be concluded. Once 'missives have been concluded' (roughly equivalent to the exchange of contracts in England), you are contractually bound to buy the property at the agreed date of entry and the seller is contractually bound to sell. The date of entry may be some weeks, or even months ahead, and it is at that point that the full purchase price is payable.

On occasions the contract provides for a deposit payable at an earlier stage but usually only in the case of a new house, where the builders tend to dictate the terms. If a deposit is required, this should be clear from the sales particulars.

From that point, your solicitor will examine the title deeds provided by the seller's solicitor and prepare the 'disposition' (the document that will transfer the ownership of the property to you), liaise with your lender, prepare the loan documents, check all the necessary searches and ensure that the seller's title matches the title plan. Your solicitor will also report to you on any title conditions that could affect the property and restrict its use, and the appropriate clause to protect your position will have been included in your offer.

These are the main features that you should look out for when buying property in Scotland. It is not as daunting as it may seem and by discussing your plans with your solicitor at an early stage you will ease the process and avoid potential pitfalls.

Buyer beware

Below are some frequently-asked questions about the Scottish system.

Q. How do I make an offer?
A. A formal offer in Scotland is submitted in writing by your solicitor. You give him instructions and he signs the offer on your behalf. You sign nothing at all except, perhaps, loan papers.

Q. Can I make an offer before I have sold my house?
A. It is possible but probably not advisable. In Scotland a contract is formed within a relatively short time. If your offer is accepted, you may find yourself in a position of having to pay the price on a particular day without having sold your own house. This is particularly disconcerting if you are used to the English system where you can pull out of a deal at the last minute. If this is likely to be difficult for you, you should not make an offer until you are certain of your own sale. It would be equally unwise to enter into an arrangement for bridging finance unless you were 100 per cent certain of your sale.

Q. Should I wait until I have had a survey carried out before submitting my offer?
A. There is no easy answer to this one. Normally a survey is carried out before the offer is submitted but if a closing date has been set (a deadline for offers to be received), then you may not have time. Your solicitor can often find out informally if the price you want to offer would be acceptable. This would be the best course of action if you want to offer less than the asking price.

Q. Is there freehold and leasehold in Scotland?
A. The system of landholding in Scotland is feudal in origin and, as owner, you will have rights, which can be passed on in perpetuity – similar to freehold. Leasehold is fairly rare for domestic properties in Scotland.

Q. What are missives?
A. When a Solicitor submits an offer for you he does so in letter form. The acceptance is also a letter. These letters form the missives. Sometimes an offer is accepted subject to certain conditions that the seller wants in the contract. This is called a 'qualified acceptance'. Once all matters are agreed, the 'bargain is concluded' and a contract is formed.

Q. Can foreigners buy Scottish property?
A. There is nothing to stop a foreigner buying Scottish property. There is no residence requirement and the property taxes are the same. Many foreigners own property from the smallest croft-house to the largest of hunting estates. Similarly, there is no reason why a foreigner cannot obtain a loan here, secured over the property, to fund part of the purchase.

Q. What is a croft?
A. Land that is registered croft land is available for anyone to purchase but an administrative body – called the Crofters Commission – regulates the occupation of crofts and may, if the land is not being properly utilised, impose a tenant upon the owner. That tenant would have rights to buy the land (but not the house if you were occupying one on the croft), usually for a very small sum.

The Crofting Acts were social engineering designed to ensure that there was land available for small-scale agricultural enterprise and to ensure that rural areas remained populated.

Buying land that is registered croft land, if it is not to be used for traditional activities such as keeping of cattle and sheep or growing crops, could result in dispossession of the land. Anyone buying and carrying out the traditional type activities should not have a problem.

If all you want to do is buy a house that has nothing beyond a garden, and it is described as a croft, there really is nothing to worry about.

Be sure to select a solicitor from the North of Scotland if you are buying a croft or crofthouse, as they tend to have more experience in this subject.

Q. What about taxes?
A. There are taxes on profits made on the sale of any property (land or buildings) that is not your main residence (Capital Gains Tax).

There is also a tax relating to residential property as opposed to bare land. This Council Tax is payable whether the house is occupied or not, and is levied on a sliding scale depending on the value (banding) of the property. The scale is different in each district and it therefore not possible to indicate the tax without knowing the property. Generally it is in the region of £1000 to £2000 per annum, but this is only a very rough guide.

Stamp duty is charged on your property at the same rates as in England and Wales. It is paid via your solicitor when you buy the property.

There is also a charge made for recording of your deeds on the Government land register, which is charged at the rate of £11 per £5,000 of value of the property.

Q. What kind of surveys are there?
A. As with England and Wales, there are three. The first is not a survey at all but a *Valuation*. It costs usually about £90 but is very limited in scope. It is usually prepared for a lender. If it is wrong you may have no comeback.

The second is a *Homebuyer's Report and Valuation*. This is much more detailed. It costs about £300 to £400. You have a direct relationship with the surveyor and if the survey is incorrect in a major way, then you will have an opportunity to make a claim on the insurance of the surveyor.

The third is a *Structural Survey*, but this is only normally instructed if the first survey indicates a serious problem. A structural survey can be quite expensive, depending upon the problem.

14 Questions, questions

This chapter deals with some typical scenarios arising from buying, selling and maintaining property.

I've been gazumped and lost money. Can I claim compensation? I recently made an offer for a house, and the seller's agent wrote to me saying his client had accepted the offer, subject to contract. I then spent money on a survey, bank costs, and legal costs. However, I later received a letter suggesting that the delay in getting a mortgage had caused the seller to 'review the situation'. Apparently he had received a higher offer but did not even give me the chance to meet it, which I would have done.

I took out a claim against the seller in the small claims court and received a letter from the seller's solicitor saying there is no claim under the Law of Property (Miscellaneous Provisions) Act 1989, where a contract is defined only in writing. Is there no recourse for costs suffered as a result of the seller's action?

The seller's solicitor is right. In these current overheated times, many people have been in this situation.

The Law of Property (Miscellaneous Provisions) Act was passed by Parliament to clarify the rules about when parties were legally bound and when they were not. It lays down certain formalities and if they are not complete, there is no binding legal relationship, and you would have no rights against the seller and vice versa.

A lockout agreement is a commonly-used way around this problem. This is a short document under which the seller agrees that, for an agreed time (such as one month), he or she will not negotiate with, or send out a contract to, anyone else. It does not commit either party to sell or buy. (For example, a buyer might not be able to raise a mortgage in time and the lockout would expire.) You should ask for a lockout agreement if you try to buy again.

I graduated four years ago, and am now studying to become a management accountant. I hope to be qualified within two years. I currently earn roughly £29k but expect my salary to rise quite a bit over the next few years. Are there any mortgage providers out there who'll take this into consideration and lend me more now? Basically, what is the most I can borrow?

With a 10 per cent deposit you could borrow up to four times your salary, so, assuming you have no outstanding loans or credit cards that could be deducted from the amount you could borrow, we are a looking at a mortgage of up to £116,000. Lenders usually do not take future earnings into consideration, but there are some who will look at affordability rather income multiples. This means you could, potentially, borrow the equivalent of four times your income with only a 5 per cent deposit. If you had a 15 per cent deposit, you could consider those lenders who offer mortgages based on 'self-certification' of income, which means that you can potentially borrow more than four times your income.

With all mortgages, and particularly self-certification, it is important to complete a monthly budget plan to make sure that you can afford the mortgage. The expectation of a large pay rise in two years may mean that all the extra expenditure of actually owning a property rather than renting, may make the mortgage too costly now. You may have a spare bedroom that you can let out and receive rent. Most lenders do not take rent into consideration, with the exception of Mortgage Express who do offer a specific 'rent-a-room' scheme that will take potential rental income into account when considering how much they would be willing to lend you. This may make all the difference to making the mortgage affordable to you.

Can taking out a loan make it more difficult to get a mortgage later? I am seriously considering consolidating debt into a loan in the region of

£10,000 over a three- to five-year period. However, I am not yet on the mortgage ladder and am concerned how a debt of this size would affect any mortgage application.

I am self-employed, have three years' good accounts and credit history and would consider buying a property in a year or two.

A loan will usually affect how much you can borrow. A lender will normally add up the monthly repayments you make on loans, and then subtract this from your income before applying the normal mortgage income multiples. These vary, but a good figure to work with is 3.25 times annual income if you are buying on your own.

Some lenders will give up to four times annual income, others work on 'affordability' models rather than income multiples (IF.com and Standard Life are among the affordability lenders). This can work out more generously for you and the flexible mortgage deals offered by these lenders are often useful for the self-employed.

How do I buy an abandoned house? In my street there is a half-built property, which has been in this state for at least 10 years. The garden is fenced, but completely overgrown. The property is not registered with the Land Registry, and the local planners have no relevant records. This house does not officially exist.

I have been made aware of the rules of 'adverse possession' under which I could assume ownership after 12 years if I erected a fence around the house and maintained it. But I don't want to wait 12 years or raise the issue locally in case somebody else claims. What can I do? I would rather buy the property legally and quickly.

If the street was originally laid out by a developer or originally belonged to a landlord who later sold on the houses, you might be able to identify the original owner from old title deeds. They could include a record of the first buyer of the house. This may not help very much if the house has changed hands, but it could give you some guidance. The County Record Office is a good place to start looking.

Also, look at the deeds of the properties next to the house, which might include agreements about garden walls or common pipes. Old Post Office directories might also give a clue.

If a person dies with no relatives and no will, that is a matter for the Treasury solicitor at Queen Anne's Chambers, 28 Broadway, London SW1H 9JS.

Is my neighbour allowed to change my wall? I had a brick-built shed along the side of my garden, with a flat roof sloping towards the next garden and a rainwater gutter next to the neighbour's property to carry away water. There was a gap of four inches between the back wall of the shed and the boundary between the properties.

I removed the shed except for the back wall and hoped my neighbour would agree to my replacing that wall with a more attractive wall without a gutter. I wanted the wall to be set back slightly in order to cover the slip of land previously overhung by the shed gutter.

The neighbour refused, citing possible claims on the strip of ground. However, without permission he has removed the guttering from the remaining shed wall and has replaced it with a layer of rendering.

The changes do not affect my property or the appearance of my wall from our side. Yet I could be said to be losing the right to keep an untidy wall with a suspended gutter on it as a bargaining counter to persuade some future owner to accept the 'complete new wall' deal. Does the neighbour have the right to 'improve' my wall?

You remain owner of the gutter. You own the air space above it as a 'flying freehold'. The neighbour had no right to remove the guttering and you have the right to require him to pay the cost of installing a new one or, if he still has the gutter he removed, he must hand it over to you as your property. As the air space belongs to you it is up to you what gutter you fix, provided it does not extend further than the four inch strip.

The neighbour has possessory rights over the four-inch strip yielded because the shed wall was not on the exact boundary. If your neighbour has used the land as a flower bed, his rights may extend up to the typical heights of the flowers or shrubs growing there over the past 12 years.

Do I have to pay for my trees to be cut if they overhang a neighbour's garden? I have tall trees in my garden with some branches above our neighbour's garden. He wants to remove them, and I have told him he is welcome to do so. However, he says that, if he employs a tree surgeon, I should give him access to my garden and pay the bill. He says he will sue me if I don't pay. Does he have the right to claim money from me?

Your neighbour is free to cut the overhanging branches but at his expense. However, the branches remain your property, and he can insist you take them back, or pay for the part of the bill that relates to their disposal.

Can I transfer a mortgage indemnity premium? In 1997, I was a first-time buyer and was charged a mortgage indemnity premium (MIP) of more than £600. This was in respect of a 25-year repayment mortgage. Can I get any of this money back if I remortgage or can the premium be transferred to another mortgage provider?

The short answer is no. There's no way to recoup the cost of this 'hidden nasty'.

The longer explanation is that a MIP is charged by some lenders when borrowers want to borrow more than 90 per cent or 95 per cent of the value of a property. The one-off fee is used to buy insurance for the lender in case the borrower doesn't pay the mortgage and the lender has to repossess the property and sell it.

According to the Council of Mortgage Lenders: 'It is not usual for the high lending fee to be refunded either in full or in part, on early redemption of a mortgage, and the nature of these policies do not usually allow them to be transferred from one loan to another.'

MIPs are less common than they were in 1997, as many lenders have abandoned them due to adverse publicity. They offer no benefit at all to borrowers and should be avoided if at all possible.

The Council of Mortgage Lenders' website is at www.cml.org.uk.

How much would I expect to pay to extend my current lease, which is 61 years? The land has recently been sold to a new freeholder and I am worried if they can charge what they like.

I have instructed my solicitor to request the rights for me to extend the lease to pass onto my buyer. My buyer wants to know how much it is to extend before she exchanges contracts.

You can try to extend your lease voluntarily by contacting the new freeholder. You will need to agree a price with him. You will probably also need to pay his solicitor's costs and your own solicitor's costs, which are likely to be about £250 plus VAT and expenses.

If the new freeholder does not agree to extend your lease voluntarily then you may have the right to insist that he gives you a lease extension. The amount that you will have to pay to the new freeholder will depend upon a number of matters, ie value of property, length of lease, ground rent etc. Also you are likely to have to pay surveyor's fees, and the legal fees are likely to be considerably higher.

What is a 'flying freehold'? My husband and I own a property each – semi-detached chalet bungalows, which are next door to each other. Both are freehold mortgaged properties. We have made a modification whereby we have 'taken' part of the loft of one to give to next door (this enables us to gain easy access to loft space and therefore create another bedroom). This now protrudes over next door by about 5ft. I understand this has created a situation known as 'flying freehold', which apparently makes a property difficult to sell and to mortgage.

Who should we get to look at the properties to assess how much of a problem this is likely to create when we want to sell? Do the building societies that hold our mortgages need to be advised at this stage?

The issue we have here is that some banks\building societies will lend on properties with flying freeholds and others will not.

Those lenders that do lend on flying freeholds will do so only in certain circumstances and, in particular, where there exists all necessary rights of support protection and entry for repair, as well as a scheme of enforceable covenants that are also such that subsequent buyers are required to enter into covenants in identical form. If this clause cannot be complied with, then the lender may proceed in any event but only if indemnity insurance is obtained and in place on completion.

I am thinking of buying a two-bedroom converted first-floor flat in a mid-terraced house. If I bought the flat, I would share the freehold with the gentleman who owns the ground-floor flat.

I am aware that flats that have share of freehold can be potentially troublesome when it comes to paying for repairs to the building (for example the roof). I asked the owner what the arrangements were and she said that, as far as she is aware, any such cost would be split two ways with the owner of the ground-floor flat. However, she did not seem certain of this.

Should there be some sort of legal agreement with whoever the freehold is shared with? If so, what should I be looking for in such an agreement? It also occurred to me that there may be potential issues with the flats and/or houses that are either side of the property (in the event of subsidence, etc). Can you give me any advice as to what I should be looking for in this respect?

It is very much better to have a share in the freehold than not. There is only a potential problem if there has not been a separate lease granted in respect of each flat – but usually there has. In any event this can easily be resolved.

An agreement can be drawn up between each owner but it is probably not necessary – in a block of two flats things can usually be agreed without too much formality. By owning a share in the freehold you will avoid any potential disputes with a freeholder and/or managing agent. Also there is no worry about extending the lease if the term is getting shorter.

Will we have problems selling our property because of old alterations? We have a through lounge, which was carried out prior to when we purchased our house some 12 years ago. Will we have problems because no building regulation consent was obtained?

Also, three years ago we had a garage erected at the bottom of our 125ft garden. We were told by the company that erected it that planning permission was not required. Is that true? Will we have problems, as we are planning to sell our property?

So far as the through lounge is concerned, you should not have any problems when you come to sell your property because the work was carried out more than 12 years ago. However, because of a recent change in the law, it may be that the solicitors acting for a buyer of your property will be concerned about the lack of building regulation consent.

If this occurs, then you can arrange for the local buildings inspector to re-inspect with a view to giving retrospective consent, or for a very modest premium, you can obtain a lack of building regulation consent indemnity policy.

So far as the garage is concerned, whether or not you require planning permission and/or building regulation consent will depend upon a number of matters, ie nature of construction, size of garage etc. We suggest that you contact your local planning authority now to find out from them their guidelines for planning permission for garages. If planning permission was required, then, again, you can apply for retrospective planning consent. Alternatively, a buyer may be prepared to proceed on the basis that the garage is now more than three years old and no enforcement proceedings have been started.

I took out a mortgage just over a year ago and it is fixed until August this year (2003) at 5.65 per cent. I would like to move house (up the ladder) at the end of the fixed term. I have just inherited some money that I could use to take 10 years off my mortgage but I still do not want to move until August 2003. Do I hold on to the money and then up it in August 2003 or re-negotiate my mortgage and pay penalties?

The answer to this really depends on two things – your tax rate and the redemption penalties. For example, let's assume your outstanding mortgage is for £50,000. If you were to pay the penalty now, and for argument's sake let's assume the penalty equates to six months' interest, then you would have to pay a penalty of £1,412 to free yourself from this mortgage.

If you opted to wait until the fixed rate period expired, and therefore put this money in some sort of savings account until then, you need to compare the amount of interest you will receive in the savings account to how much interest you would pay on the mortgage (also taking into account the assumed £1,412 you would have to pay to redeem the mortgage). This is where your tax rate comes into the equation. Because interest on a savings account is taxed, it will make a difference to your decision if you are a higher-rate tax payer.

I suggest you consult an independent financial adviser. With access to the full details they would be able to make an informed decision as to which option is most financially suitable to you.

I earn about £15,000 a year and would like to buy my own place. What is on offer for such a low wage?

You could potentially borrow up to four times your gross salary, therefore assuming you earn £15,000 before tax, you could potentially borrow £60,000.

If we also assume you have savings that amount to a 10 per cent deposit you could potentially buy a property worth £66,000. This may well be enough depending on where and what you want to buy. However, it is based on a number of assumptions such as you having no outstanding debt that could reduce your borrowing power, you have saved up at least a 10 per cent deposit and also have extra money to cover your purchase costs.

In order to increase your borrowing power there are other options that you could consider, such as lenders who base their decision on a borrower's affordability rather than set income multiples, or lenders who offer 100 per cent mortgages, thus negating the need for a deposit.

I suggest you seek independent advice to see if any of these options are suitable for you. With more information to work on, an independent adviser should be able to work out the best option for you, including whether you should be thinking of buying at all.

Is it possible to obtain a joint 100 per cent mortgage, ie with no deposit? A flatmate and I are considering a joint mortgage application to avoid wasting money on rent. I have money for a deposit, my flatmate does not.

In this instance, and for simplicity, can a joint 100 per cent mortgage be obtained? We are both in permanent employment.

It is possible for you both to get a 100 per cent mortgage but the bigger issue here is ensuring you both understand exactly what you are about to undertake. While friends buying together has become a more popular way for first-time buyers to get on the property ladder as prices soar, you both need to be aware of the risks involved before committing to buying a property together.

The main risk is what will happen if one of you decides to move out, falls on hard times or even dies. All parties on the mortgage deed will be jointly and severally liable to pay the mortgage, and if any of these scenarios should happen, it may fall on the other co-owner to make up the balance of the mortgage payments. Whether or not the increased payments are manageable may depend on how far down the line this happens, as financial circumstances will obviously change over time.

A good safeguard is to draw up a legal agreement to cover these eventualities before the purchase is completed. It should take into account how much you are both putting into the property, both in terms of any deposit you initially put down and the various costs of purchase.

Although only one of you has money for a deposit I still think it is worthwhile using it for this purpose, as long as it is at least 5 per cent of the purchase price. This is because it will enable you to choose from a much wider range of lenders and mortgages, and consequently you will both benefit by being able to get a lower interest rate. Although, as far as the lender is concerned you will both be equally responsible for making the mortgage payments but you can, if you wish, split the payments unevenly between yourselves if, for example, you provide all of the deposit. This is one of the reasons why it is so important for you both to agree in writing beforehand what proportion of the mortgage and household bills you each pay and how the proceeds will be split if and when you sell. This should ensure that there is no dispute in the future as to what each party is entitled to if and when it comes to buying a co-owner out or selling the property.

You should both independently seek advice from a solicitor (and this should not be the same solicitor, although two solicitors from the same firm would be OK) before you commit to anything.

We are buying a brand new house and we are trying to sort out our finances. We want to know whether or not we can have a mortgage offer now, which will be valid for our purchase even though the house will not be completed for another six months.

Yes, you can. Most mortgage offers are valid for a period of three to six months, so this may mean that you will have to renew your offer, which typically involves the lender getting an updated credit search and proof of your earnings. Be mindful though because even though you may chose a particular mortgage deal now, it may have expired by the time your house is ready. You should take care to check this with the lender, as some schemes have deadlines by which the mortgage must be drawn down.

I live in a Victorian house with cellars that I would like to use for extra living space. The cellars themselves are not totally underground. Only about 4ft of the cellars are. I have put windows in and I am putting in forced-air ventilation to the outside. The cellars have asphalt floors and the walls have been dampcoursed. There are only two walls that give me cause for concern, because they back on to the front gardens and only the bottom 4ft has signs of damp. All the other walls are fine.

I don't really want to dig out the front gardens and treat the walls from the outside because that would be very time-consuming and impractical. Can I treat the problem walls from the inside to stop damp and the smell of damp from penetrating inside. I have been advised to apply rot-proof roofing felt bonded with cold asphalt to the affected walls and continued to the floor to give an effective seal. Would this work? Are there any other alternatives? I did apply Cellar Paint to the walls some years ago but that has peeled off.

What you have to bear in mind is that any below-ground walls will always be prone to lateral groundwater penetration. Tanking the walls on the inside may stop the water showing on the decorative surfaces, but the brickwork itself will still be saturated, and the moisture will be trapped behind the tanking. This usually results in humid, smelly conditions.

The first thing you should do is to find out why the front walls are wetter than the others. It may be that the rainwater downpipe from the roof is not connected up to the main drains, but is discharging into the ground. Victorian houses often had two separate drainage systems, with foul water (sewage) going into the drains, and rainwater going into 'soakaways', which were holes in the ground next to the basement walls. It may be that diverting this water away to the drains will solve 90 per cent of your dampness problems.

After that, digging a trench and waterproofing the wall on the outside is by far the best option. But if you really want to try and keep the water at bay from the inside, then you need a drained ventilated membrane system such as Platon (from Triton Chemicals Ltd, 020 8310 3929) or Newlath (from John Newton & Co, 020 7237 1217). These can be finished internally by plastering or panelling.

I'd like to have a shower in my bathroom but the water pressure is very low upstairs. Are there any ways round this?

You don't say whether you are talking about low mains pressure or low pressure from a storage tank. If the former, then the first thing to do is check with your water supplier what the pressure should be in your area, and that you are not restricting this with narrow-bore pipework. But the usual problem in upstairs bathrooms is that the water storage tank is only a few centimetres higher than the shower outlet, giving only a small 'head' of pressure. Again, you should first check that the pipes are not blocked or scaled up, and that the hot and cold feeds from the tank to the bathroom (including the hot flow through the heater or cylinder) are all in 22mm pipe, rather than 15mm.

Assuming all these are in order, and the pressure is still low, then the answer is to fit an electric shower booster pump. These can be either twin-port – boosting both hot and cold supplies from the existing plumbing system – or single-port, which will provide a boosted cold supply for an 'instant' electric shower unit. These are fairly simple devices, and can be fitted by keen DIYers, but if you are not confident of your plumbing skills, you would be well advised to have the pump fitted by a professional plumbing and heating engineer, and the electrics should be installed or approved by an NICEIC registered electrician.

We live in a 1920s semi and every year gusts of wind dislodge one or two roof slates. The roof is in its original 1920s condition with no underfelt. There are adverts in the papers for a 'foam spray solution' for old roofs. These are guaranteed for 20 or so years. Is this the easiest way forward, or should we look to get the whole roof redone? I have heard conflicting reports about the foam-type repair, varying from 'fantastic' to 'waste of money'. As the damage is only slight each year, would it be better to just keep on repairing the occasional damage instead?

The fact that slates are slipping every year indicates that the nails which hold them to the timber battens are rusted through, and it is time to have the roof stripped off and re-covered. Having foam sprayed onto the undersides of the slates may sound like a wonderful high-tech solution but it is a bad idea. It is at odds with the recommendations of the Building Regulations, which require a clear 50 mm ventilated gap between insulation and roof covering. The foam sets hard and removes the two vital attributes of a traditional roof, which are the ability to breathe and to move. The foam covers the battens and the top surfaces of the rafters, which could lead to them rot. It also sticks tight to the slates and makes it almost impossible for them to ever be re-used. You will also probably find that the cost of the spray-on foam solution will be three or four times that of having the roof re-covered in the traditional way. Try to find a roofer who will remove the existing slates carefully and re-use as many as possible.

Several of my double-glazed windows have misted up between the panes. The double-glazing was already installed when I bought the house and the estate agent's particulars implied that this was a good thing. But on the south-facing side of the house (overlooking the garden), on a sunny day, I can hardly see out of the windows because of the misting. Is there anything that can be done to cure this, or, if I have the double-glazing replaced, is there any way of ensuring that it does not happen in the future?

Sealed double-glazed units (SGUs) are always prone to misting up. Manufacturers postpone the inevitable by incorporating a desiccant material in the perforated alloy strip that runs around the edges between the two panes of glass. But eventually the desiccant will become saturated, and then misting is inevitable. How long this takes depends upon a number of factors – if the SGUs are manufactured and installed to the correct British Standards, then they should last at least 20 years. But for this to happen, the SGUs must be mounted in drained, ventilated rebates in the window frames, so that no moisture is allowed to come into contact with the edges of the glass. Unfortunately, most 'double-glazing' is supplied and installed by companies who do not understand these principles, and SGUs are often fixed tight into PVCU frames or even sealed in with mastic or putty into timber or alloy frames. In these circumstances misting can occur within a few years, or even months of installation.

I live in a basement flat in a Victorian house and am besieged by noise – traffic outside, music from either side, and the footsteps of the people upstairs. What can I do to make my life quieter?

The best way to cut down traffic noise is to fit secondary glazing. This is not to be confused with double-glazing, which has a 3 or 4mm air gap between the two panes of glass, and is good for thermal insulation. Secondary glazing has a much bigger air gap – 200mm is the optimum – and will reduce traffic noise by up to two-thirds. For best results, make sure you thoroughly draught-proof the existing windows at the same time, as air-borne sound travels through gaps.

Something of the same philosophy applies to noise from your next-door neighbours – if you can smell their cooking then you will also be able to hear their TV – so locating and plugging gaps in the party walls can do a lot to cut down unwanted noise intrusion.

The most difficult problem is the footsteps from the neighbours above. Ideally, this involves constructing a new floor – separated by sound-proofing quilt – on top of the existing floor in their flat. A less satisfactory alternative is to build a false ceiling in the lower flat. You can download information on improving sound insulation from the Building Research Establishment website.

Last winter I had trouble with frozen pipes and water tanks in my roof space. How can I make sure this does not happen again, and are there any other precautions that I should take when the cold weather approaches?

Pipes and tanks freezing in roof spaces is an inevitable result of the high levels of insulation that we now have in our homes. Water tanks are kept up in the loft because it is a convenient place to have them, and because the height provides a good head of pressure that allows water to flow by gravity to kitchen and bathroom taps. But because most homes now have a thick layer of insulation quilt between the top-floor ceiling joists, very little heat escapes up into the roof space, and so on cold winter nights the temperature can easily fall below freezing.

Apart from the inconvenience of having the water supply cut off, the main problem with freezing water is that as it freezes it also expands, and so can damage the plumbing. The resulting leak is often inaccurately referred to as a 'burst pipe', but a burst or split in a straight run of copper pipe is rare. What usually happens is that the expanding ice pushes compression joints open – such as those that connect pipes to tanks. Should this happen, by the way, you should always check to see whether the fitting can be pushed back into place and re-tightened, before panicking and calling out the emergency plumber.

Preventing this situation is achieved by making sure that loft insulation goes over, rather than under, pipes and tanks, thus keeping them at house temperature. If this is not possible, then a small electric heater with a 'frost' setting on the thermostat can be set up in the loft.

Other weak points are outside taps and lavatory cisterns. These should be isolated by cheap on/off valves ('ball-o-fix' or similar), which can be turned on and off with a screwdriver. Turn them off when freezing weather threatens, and leave the taps open and cisterns empty until warm conditions return.

15 Useful contacts

Property websites

www.asserta.co.uk

www.easier.co.uk

www.findaproperty.com

www.fish4homes.co.uk

www.homebankplc.com

www.homes-on-line.com

www.homecheck.co.uk

www.homepages.co.uk

www.home-sale.co.uk

www.hometrack.co.uk

www.houseweb.co.uk

www.new-homes.co.uk

www.propertymarket.co.uk

www.propertyfinder.co.uk

www.propertyworld.co.uk

www.rightmove.co.uk

www.thisislondon.co.uk

www.upmystreet.co.uk

Mortgage websites

www.homebankplc.com

www.about-mortgages.co.uk

www.charcolonline.co.uk

www.moneyfacts.co.uk

www.moneysupermarket.co.uk

www.yourmortgage.co.uk

Organisations

Architectural Association
36 Bedford Square
London WC1B 3ES
Tel: 020 7887 4000
Fax: 020 7414 0782
Website: www.arch-assoc.org.uk

Architecture and Surveying Institute
St Mary House
15A St Mary Street
Chippenham
Wiltshire SN15 3WD
Tel: 01249 444505
Fax: 01249 443602
Website: www.asi.org.uk

Association of British Insurers
51 Gresham Street
London EC2V 7HQ
Tel: 020 7600 3333
Fax: 020 7696 8999
Website: www.abi.org.uk

Association of Building Engineers
Lutyens House
Billing Brook Road
Weston Favell
Northampton NN3 8NW
Tel: 01604 404121
Fax: 01604 784220

Association of Plumbing and Heating Contractors
Ensign House
Ensign Business Centre
Westwood Way
Coventry CV4 8JA
Tel: 0800 542 6060
Fax: 024 7647 0942
Website: www.licensedplumber.co.uk

Association of Relocation Agents
PO Box 189
Diss
Norfolk IP22 1PE
Tel: 08700 737475
Fax: 08700 718719
Website: www.relocationagents.com

The Association of Residential Managing Agents
Tel: 020 7978 2607
Website: www.arma.org.uk

The Association of Residential Letting Agents
Tel: 0845 345 5752
Website: www.arla.co.uk

The Association of Building Engineers
Tel: 01604 404 121
Website: www.abe.org.uk

British Association of Removers
3 Churchill Court
58 Station Road
North Harrow
Middlesex HA2 7SA
Tel: 020 8861 3331
Fax: 020 8861 3332
Website: www.barmovers.com

British Insurance Brokers' Association
BIBA House
14 Bevis Marks
London EC3A 7NT
Tel: 020 7623 9043
Fax: 020 7626 9676
Website: www.biba.org.uk

Building Societies Association
3 Savile Row
London W1S 3PB
Tel: 020 7437 0655
Fax: 020 7734 6416
Website: www.bsa.org.uk

Construction Confederation
Construction House
56–64 Leonard Street
London EC2A 4JX
Tel: 020 7608 5000
Fax: 020 7608 5001
Website: www.thecc.org.uk

The Controller of Stamps
London Stamp Office
South West Wing
Bush House
Strand
London WC2B 4QN
Tel: Helpline 0845 6030 135
Fax: 020 7438 7302
Website: www.inlandrevenue.gov.uk/so

Council for Licensed Conveyancers
16 Glebe Road
Chelmsford
Essex CM1 1QG
Tel: 01245 349599
Fax: 01245 341300
Website: www.conveyancer.org.uk

Council for Registered Gas Installers (CORGI)
Unit 1 Elmwood
Chineham Park
Basingstoke
Hampshire RG24 8WG
Tel: 01256 372200
Fax: 01256 708144
Website: www.corgi-gas.com

Council of Mortgage Lenders
3 Savile Row
London W1S 3PB
Tel: 020 7437 0075
Fax: 020 7434 3791
Website: www.cml.org.uk

Electrical Contractors' Association
ESCA House
34 Palace Court
London W2 4HY
Tel: 020 7313 4800
Fax: 020 7221 7344
Website: www.eca.co.uk

English Heritage
Customer Services Department
PO Box 569
Swindon SN2 2YP
Tel: 0870 333 1181
Fax: 01793 414926
Website: www.english-heritage.org.uk

Federation of Master Builders
14–15 Great James Street
London WC1N 3DP
Tel: 020 7242 7583
Fax: 020 7404 0296
Website: www.fmb.org.uk

Independent Financial Advisors Promotion
Tel: 0800 085 3250
Website: www.ifap.org.uk

The Institute of Plumbing
64 Station Lane
Hornchurch
Essex RM12 6NB
Tel: 01708 472791
Fax: 01708 448987
Website: www.plumbers.org.uk

The Law Commission
Conquest House
37–38 John Street
Theobalds Road
London WC1N 2BQ
Tel: 020 7453 1220
Fax: 020 7453 1297
Website: www.lawcom.gov.uk

The Law Society
113 Chancery Lane
London WC2A 1PL
Tel: 020 7242 1222
Fax: 020 7831 0344
Website: www.lawsociety.org.uk

The Law Society of Scotland
26 Drumsheugh Gardens
Edinburgh EH3 7YR
Tel: 0131 226 7411
Fax: 0131 225 2934
Website: www.lawscot.org.uk

Legal Services Ombudsman
1st Floor
Sunlight House
Quay Street
Manchester M3 3JZ
Tel: 0161 839 7262
Fax: 0161 832 5446
Website: www.olso.org

National Approval Council for Security Systems (NACOSS)
Queensgate House, 14 Cookham Road
Maidenhead
Berkshire SL6 8AJ
Tel: 01628 637512
Fax: 01628 773367
Website: www.nsi.org.uk

The National Association of Estate Agents (NAEA)
Arbon House, 21 Jury Street
Warwick
Warwickshire CV34 4EH
Tel: 01926 496800
Fax: 01926 400953
Website: www.propertylive.co.uk

National Federation of Builders
Construction House, 56–64 Leonard Street
London EC2A 4JX
Tel: 020 7608 5150
Fax: 020 7608 5151
Website: www.builders.org.uk

National Guild of Removers and Storers
3 High Street
Chesham
Buckinghamshire HP5 1BG
Tel: 01494 792279
Fax: 01494 792111
Website: www.ngrs.co.uk

National House Building Council (NHBC)
Buildmark House, Chiltern Avenue
Amersham
Buckinghamshire HP6 5AP
Tel: 01494 434477
Fax: 01494 735201
Website: www.nhbc.co.uk

National Land Information Services
Tel: 01279 451 625
Website: www.nlis.org.uk

New Homes Marketing Board (NHMB)
56–64 Leonard Street
London EC2A 4JX
Tel: 020 7608 5100
Fax: 020 7608 5101
Website: www.new-homes.co.uk

Office of the Deputy Prime Minister
Housing Private Sector Division
Website: www.odpm.gov.uk

Office of the Ombudsman for Estate Agents (OEA)
Beckett House
4 Bridge Street
Salisbury
Wiltshire SP1 2LX
Tel: 01722 333306
Fax: 01722 332296
Website: www.org.co.uk

Office for the Supervision of Solicitors (OSS)
Victoria Court
8 Dormer Place
Leamington Spa
Warwickshire CV32 5AE
Tel: 01926 820082
Fax: 01926 431435
Website: www.lawsociety.org.uk

Registry of County Court Judgements
Registry Trust Ltd
173–175 Cleveland Street
London W1P 5PE
Tel: 020 7380 0133

The Royal Incorporation of Architects in Scotland (RIA Scotland)
15 Rutland Square
Edinburgh EH1 2BE
Tel: 0131 229 7545
Fax: 0131 228 2188
Website: www.rias.org.uk

Royal Institute of British Architects (RIBA)
Client Services
66 Portland Place
London W1B 1AD
Tel: 020 7580 5533
Fax: 020 7255 1541
Website: www.architecture.com

Royal Institution of Chartered Surveyors (RICS)
RICS Contact Centre
Surveyor Court
Westwood Way
Coventry CV4 8JE
Tel: 0870 333 1600
Website: www.rics.org.uk

Royal Institution of Chartered Surveyors in Scotland (RICS Scotland)
9 Manor Place
Edinburgh EH3 7DN
Tel: 0131 225 7078
Fax: 0131 240 0830
Website: www.rics-scotland.org.uk

Royal Society of Architects in Wales
Bute Building
King Edward VII Avenue
Cathays Park
Cardiff CF10 3NB
Tel: 029 2087 4753
Fax: 029 2087 4926
Website: www.architecture-wales.com

Royal Society of Ulster Architects (RSUA)
2 Mount Charles
Belfast BT7 1NZ
Tel: 028 9032 3760
Fax: 028 9023 7313
Website: www.rsua.org.uk

Royal Town Planning Institute
41 Botolph Lane
London EC3R 8DL
Tel: 020 7929 9494
Fax: 020 7929 9490
Website: www.rtpi.org.uk

Scottish Building
Carron Grange
Carrongrange Avenue
Stenhousemuir FK5 3BQ
Tel: 01324 555550
Fax: 01324 555551
Website: www.scottish-building.co.uk

The Scottish Civic Trust
The Tobacco Merchants House
42 Miller Street
Glasgow G1 1DT
Tel: 0141 221 1466
Fax: 0141 248 6952
Website www.scotnet.co.uk/sct

The Society for the Protection of Ancient Buildings
37 Spital Square
London E1 6DY
Tel: 020 7377 1644
Fax: 020 7247 5296
Website www.spab.org.uk

The Stationary Office (TSO)
Duke Street
PO Box 29
Norwich NR3 1GN
Tel: 0870 600 5522
Fax: 0870 600 5533
Website: www.tso.co.uk

Trading Standards Office
Website: www.tradingstandards.gov.uk

Zurich Municipal
Galaxy House
Southwood Crescent
Farnborough
Hampshire GU14 0NJ
Tel: 01252 522000
Fax: 01252 372989
Website: www.zurich.com

Index

Index

Index of advertisers

240